TEACH ME
HOW TO
PROSPER

Books by Kynan Bridges

Releasing Miracles

Teach Me How to Prosper

TEACH ME
HOW TO
PROSPER

BIBLICAL KEYS TO
SUPERNATURAL
ABUNDANCE

KYNAN BRIDGES

Chosen
a division of Baker Publishing Group
Minneapolis, Minnesota

© 2024 by Kynan Bridges

Published by Chosen Books
Minneapolis, Minnesota
ChosenBooks.com

Printed in the United States of America

Library of Congress Cataloging-in-Publication Data
Names: Bridges, Kynan, author.
Title: Teach me how to prosper : Biblical keys to supernatural abundance / Kynan Bridges.
Description: Minneapolis, Minnesota : Chosen Books, a division of Baker Publishing Group, [2024] | Includes bibliographical references.
Identifiers: LCCN 2024010290 | ISBN 9780800762612 (paper) | ISBN 9780800772857 (casebound) | ISBN 9781493447305 (ebook)
Subjects: LCSH: Wealth—Religious aspects—Christianity. | Wealth—Biblical teaching.
Classification: LCC BR115.W4 B753 2024 | DDC 241/.68—dc23/eng/20240328
LC record available at https://lccn.loc.gov/2024010290

Cover design by Rob Williams, Inside Out Creative Arts

Baker Publishing Group publications use paper produced from sustainable forestry practices and postconsumer waste whenever possible.

24   25   26   27   28   29   30   7   6   5   4   3   2   1

I dedicate this book to the Lord Jesus, the One through whom I am able to pen this impactful message. I dedicate this book to the millions of people who are searching for more, and the tens of millions who need to have an introduction to Jehovah Jireh, the God who provides and prospers. I dedicate this book to my beautiful wife of my youth, Gloria Bridges. You are my "Sugar Boo"; you are my Queen. I dedicate this book to my six beautiful children; you inspire me. To my wonderful church family and ministry partners, you have helped to get this and many other messages into the hands of those whose lives are being transformed by its contents.

CONTENTS

Foreword   9

1. God's Purpose for Prosperity   13
2. Even as Your Soul Prospers   25
3. Poverty, the Destiny Thief   41
4. The Joseph Mandate   56
5. Real versus False Prosperity   70
6. The Power of the Blessing   84
7. The Law of Seedtime and Harvest and Cooperating with the Spirit of Divine Increase   100
8. Tired of Being Sick and Tired and Renouncing the Vow of Poverty   118
9. Seeking First the Kingdom of God   130
10. Why Am I Broke? Asking the *Hard* Questions   141
11. The Love of Money . . .   158
12. Prospering in the End Times   169

Acknowledgments   181
Notes   183

FOREWORD

As I've watched the pendulum swing in the body of Christ concerning the "prosperity gospel," I've stood amazed. Clearly there have been abuses and even false teaching associated with it. However, this does not detract from the truth of God's Word. He desires us to prosper and increase in every dimension, including our finances.

In my estimation, the attack against the financial prosperity of the saints is the work of the enemy, who desires to condemn and diminish the message of prosperity among the people of God. He wants to make us believe that the desire to have wealth is carnal and nonspiritual. If he can propagate this idea, then he can thwart the purposes of God. Deuteronomy 8:18 lets us know that the power to get wealth is an essential part of God's will being done in the earth.

The covenant intent of God's will being done in the earth requires people who have wealth. Someone has to finance the physical manifestation of heaven coming to earth. Without prosperity, we can never see a societal effect of the gospel. This requires money, and a lot of it. This money will always come through the people of God. Even in the wilderness, God used His people, whom He had just brought out of Egypt. Remember that they had asked of the Egyptians their wealth. In amazement, the people of Egypt had given them the riches and sent them away. Therefore, when it came time to build God a dwelling place in the wilderness, everything they needed came through the people of God. Exodus 36:5–7 shows that the people had so much wealth that Moses had to restrain them from giving too much.

The main point I'm making is that the wealth, materials, and riches required to build the tabernacle came *through* the people. This is always the desire and intent of the Lord. He wants to bless His people so much that we have everything we need and even want, plus the ability to fulfill His work as well. This means we are to be a people of prosperity. Don't let anyone controlled by the religious spirit make you believe otherwise. You are ordained and commissioned to prosper.

The apostle Paul told Timothy (1 Timothy 6:17–19) how the wealthy were to steward their riches: 1.) Don't trust in it. Our trust and confidence are to always be in God. 2.) Do good with it. We are to advance the kingdom of God and bless others with it. 3.) Enjoy it. God gives us richly all things to enjoy. He loves to see His people blessed and living a good life. Don't allow anyone to steal this from you. This isn't selfish. This is God-ordained.

My dear friend Kynan Bridges explains this and more in this wonderful book. He unveils principles that are necessary to prosper and handle prosperity. Like when

Isaac sowed into the land (see Genesis 26:12–14), he not only prospered, he kept prospering. God so blessed and increased him that the Philistines of the land envied him. God desires to make His covenant people such an example of wealth and prosperity that it amazes those who don't know Him. You and I can be some of these people. As we allow ourselves to be taught how to prosper, this will be our portion and lot in life. Prosperity is not an accident. It is a result of purposeful activity in agreement with God's Word. May the Holy Spirit take the words of this book and help you to prosper. The result will be living a new kind of life and empowering the purposes of God in the earth. I'm ready—how about you?

Robert Henderson
Bestselling author, THE COURTS OF HEAVEN series

GOD'S PURPOSE FOR PROSPERITY

> Then God blessed them, and God said to them, "Be fruit-
> ful and multiply; fill the earth and subdue it; have domin-
> ion over the fish of the sea, over the birds of the air, and
> over every living thing that moves on the earth."
>
> —Genesis 1:28

The garden was lush with a clean atmosphere. The pal-
pable presence of God permeated the air. The man and
the woman were oblivious to the concept of lack, insufficiency, and poverty. God commanded them to be fruitful
and multiply—He commanded them to prosper.

The truth is, the principle of prosperity is not the invention of a televangelist or an American business mogul.
Prosperity was, and is, God's idea. That's right! God desires that the human race prospers. This concept may seem

controversial to some, but let us consider what the Bible says in Genesis 1:28 above.

The word *fruitful* here comes from the Hebrew word *pārâ*, which means "to bear fruit."[1] God designed us to be fruitful in every area of our lives. This word also implies increase. We were created to experience increase. Anything that doesn't increase is not functioning according to God's purpose, His specific command to bear fruit.

God wanted the human race to reproduce after its kind because the human race was made in the image of God. The more humans reproduced, the more the earth looked like God. This is why the enemy sought to introduce sin into the world because sin brings barrenness, which is antithetical to the nature of God. The more sin, the more barren the earth would become. Barrenness is unnatural.

Let's look at the word *fruitfulness* more in depth. *Oxford English Dictionary* defines *fruitful* as "producing good or helpful results; productive," and *Merriam-Webster Dictionary* includes the meaning of "offspring."[2] This word originates from the Latin word *fertilis*, which means "fertile or fertilizing."[3] In other words, God created mankind and put within them the fertilizer necessary to expand His abundance into every sphere of society.

The Purpose for Prosperity

God had a plan. He wanted human beings to be His ambassadors on earth. Mankind was designed and fashioned in the image of God, and as image bearers, humankind was called to establish His kingdom and advance His agenda on earth. In fact, Adam and Eve and all humankind were intended to spread the atmosphere of the garden of Eden across every conceivable sphere of the planet.

If God designed human beings to be fertile, abundant, productive, and fruitful, when and where did poverty, lack, and barrenness come into the picture? Poverty and lack came into the earth as a result of the curse, and the curse came about as a result of sin. When Adam and Eve ate the fruit from the Tree of Knowledge of Good and Evil, they unleashed a spiritual cancer called sin that began to corrupt the very fabric of the world. Their sin didn't simply affect them; it actually affected the entire human race and all of creation. Sin turned the world upside down. Faith was replaced with fear. Confidence in God was replaced with self-righteousness and spiritual insecurity. True worship was replaced with man-made religion. For the first time in mankind's existence, they experienced guilt, shame, and condemnation.

In Genesis 3, we see the implication of sin in the curse God pronounced over humanity.

> Then to Adam He said, "Because you have heeded the voice of your wife, and have eaten from the tree of which I commanded you, saying, 'You shall not eat of it':
>
> "Cursed is the ground for your sake;
> In toil you shall eat of it
> All the days of your life.
> Both thorns and thistles it shall bring forth for you,
> And you shall eat the herb of the field.
> In the sweat of your face you shall eat bread
> Till you return to the ground,
> For out of it you were taken;

For dust you are,
And to dust you shall return."

—Genesis 3:17–19

Notice what the Scripture says, "Cursed is the ground for your sake . . ." This implies that the power of sin not only hindered man's fellowship with God, but it actually hindered his relationship with the earth. The ground that once yielded its fruit to Adam and Eve was no longer in cooperation with them but instead was barren and stubborn and could only be tilled through toil.

We must understand that toiling is a part of the curse. Before humankind fell, Adam tilled the ground from a posture of rest and peace. Adam worked, but he did not toil. The word *toil* is defined as "exhausting physical labor or to work extremely hard or incessantly."[4] It was never God's plan for human beings to struggle or be oppressed by lack and poverty.

The Power of Stewardship

In the book of Genesis, God gave Adam stewardship over the garden of Eden. He was called to "dress and to keep it." What did this mean? The Hebrew word for *dress* there is the word ʿābad, which means "to work or to serve."[5] The other word used in this passage is the word *keep*. This is from the Hebrew word šāmar, which means to "keep, guard, observe, or give heed."[6]

Another word used to describe this term is *celebrate* (as in celebrating the feast days). This is very powerful! Adam was called by God to steward the garden of Eden with a sense of stewardship or celebration. He was happy and joyful in his work. He wasn't waiting to clock off from work because of stress or exhaustion. Instead, Adam actually worked from a posture of rest. This was God's original design and was God's plan not just for Adam but for the entire human race. Understanding the purpose and law of stewardship is essential to understanding and walking in biblical prosperity.

God never establishes anything in the earth without a steward. In the garden of Eden, mankind were the legal stewards of that environment. This is why the serpent came to tempt Eve in the garden; he was after the legal custody of the garden of Eden. Unfortunately, due to sin, mankind gave up their custodianship to the devil, and so began the spiritual and physical decline of the earth. God is a God of stewardship, and He abides by three main laws of stewardship:

A. We cannot be trusted with resources we don't have the capacity to steward.

B. God will not give you more if you have shown an inability to manage what you have.

C. God holds us accountable for what He places in our care.

We have been called by God to steward the resources He has entrusted to us. God did not create you to toil. It is not His will that you struggle for money or that you live hand to mouth. You are probably asking yourself, *But what about all the poverty in the world today?* That is a great question. The truth is that the world is not suffering from a lack of resources; the world is suffering from *poor stewardship.*

Sin released a curse that has caused selfishness, greed, and abuse to proliferate throughout the world. Children are hungry in so-called third-world countries, not because of a deficiency in natural materials, but because of bad governance and poor stewardship. Some countries have more natural resources than any other place in the world, but their citizens can't even afford a bag of rice. Why? Sin not only separates people from God, but it separates people from His purpose and provision. The late Dr. Myles Munroe would often say, "Where purpose is not known, abuse is inevitable."[7]

Many years ago, on my first-ever mission trip, I went to West Africa. Upon arrival, I was shocked at the level of poverty that I witnessed firsthand. There was no running water or functional plumbing. There were no microwaves; everything that I ate was prepared over a fire with hot coals. Even my clothes were ironed with a hot iron that used coal. This region has more gold and diamonds than almost any country in the world, yet the people were in abject poverty.

I sat with a group of pastors who represented over twenty churches in the area and asked them what their biggest need was for their ministries; they all said, without hesitation or equivocation, "Money!" Although the answer seemed so obvious, I was actually very surprised. At that moment, I realized the self-righteous narrative that I held for so many years that "It's not about money!" was not only false, it was self-centered and demonic.

These pastors loved God and were leading their local churches to the best of their abilities, but they were being oppressed financially. They told me that they couldn't compete with the local mosque that possessed more resources. This wasn't because their country was physically barren; this was because the curse had not been broken. That's right! In the same manner, thousands, if not millions, of people are operating under a curse of barrenness because they do not know that it is the will of God for them to be blessed.

My encounters in Africa gave me a totally different perspective on wealth and poverty. I realized that it was easier to hyper-spiritualize the problems of the less fortunate because it gave me a comfortable excuse. As long as I made everything spiritual and ignored the pragmatic aspects of the gospel and the kingdom of God, I didn't have to face the poverty mindset which I justified through spirituality. (We will discuss the poverty mentality in a later chapter.)

The Mind of God

Earlier, we mentioned that prosperity is God's idea. The word *prosperity* was invented by God. This is not the invention of a televangelist as many would assume. If prosperity was created and established by God, then it means that He has a specific intention for His children. God intended for His creation to prosper so that His plans could be carried out.

Deuteronomy 8:18 says, "And you shall remember the LORD your God, for it is He who gives you power to get wealth, that He may establish His covenant which He swore to your fathers, as it is this day." When the ancient Israelites were entering the Promised Land, God reminded them that it was He who brought them out of Egypt and who gave them the power to obtain wealth. The purpose of wealth is laid out in the same verse: "to establish His covenant that he swore to your fathers."

The word *power* in this verse comes from the Hebrew word *kōaḥ*, which means "power, strength, or might"; it also means the "strength of God and angels."[8] In other words, God told the Israelites that in order to establish His covenant, they would need wealth, and in order to obtain this wealth, they would need supernatural empowerment. I don't believe that it is any coincidence that the Jewish community is one of the wealthiest in the world to this day because they believe the promise that God made to them.

A dear friend of mine has been in the financial planning business for almost thirty years. One day, he told me a great story. He said that he was speaking to one of his wealthy Jewish colleagues. He asked him a very interesting question. "Between your Christian and Jewish clients, who do you find to be wealthier?"

The man answered, "My Jewish clients by far!" Then the financial planner explained why. "You Christians tend to live from the back of the book, and we Jewish people tend to live from the front of the book." He was referring to the Old Testament promises. You will find that most of the financial promises are in the Old Testament.

This is not some antisemitic rhetoric about the Jewish community. This is not about inherent frugality or any genetic predisposition toward wealth. In fact, there are both poor Jews and Christians. Instead, this has to do with believing that God wants you to be prosperous. It is difficult to receive blessings from God when you believe that blessings are bad or sinful. When God spoke to the Israelites of old, He told them that He would give them "the power to get wealth." There is a mystery in that statement that every believer must understand, especially as we approach increasingly perilous times. Money empowers decisions. This is a very key principle when it comes to understanding God's plan to prosper His people. In order to do what we have been called to do, we need both spiritual and natural resources. How can you build churches without money? How can you send missionaries to remote communities without money? How can you train pastors and leaders without money? How can you broadcast the gospel of Christ without money?

Wealth is not the accumulation of things; it is the accumulation of means. The Tower of Babel is a perfect example of this truth. Babylon was able to build a tower that had the potential to reach the heavens because the people were united and they possessed the resources. They were able to finance their agenda. Whoever possesses the means has the ability to establish their agenda. This is why we see so many demonic agendas propagated in the earth today. Wealth in the hands of wicked men leads to the furtherance of wicked agendas. Wealth in the hands of righteous men leads to the furtherance of righteous agendas. It depends on whose hand the wealth is in. The wealth of the wicked is laid up for the righteous. (See Proverbs 13:22.) When we are aligned with God's purposes (to expand, to establish, to empower), we are prepared to prosper.

Prosperity Follows Purpose

It is critical for us to understand the heart and mind of God when it comes to the subject of prosperity. God has a purpose for prosperity, and prosperity always follows that purpose. God will *never* prosper something that doesn't have a purpose. The why is always more important than the how. Until I understood this truth, my life seemed to be stagnant. I was angry and frustrated with God.

One night, I was so exacerbated that I yelled at the sky and demanded that God tell me what He wanted from me. At the time, I was struggling to pay bills and provide for my wife and children. I was so vulnerable and desperate that I didn't know what else to do. After I cried out to God, I simply lay on the ground and waited on God to answer me. Suddenly, the still, small voice of God spoke to me. He said, "I want you!" I was a bit perplexed. Then He spoke again. "I want you!"

The only thing I knew to respond was, "Lord, here I am! I surrender to you!" Something broke inside me. I finally said yes to God's purpose for my life.

I got off the ground and went inside my house. My wife asked me where I had been. I said, "Talking to the Lord!" I felt a shift in the atmosphere. The next morning, I received an unexpected check in the mail for one thousand dollars. I was reminded of Deuteronomy 1:11, when God told the Israelites that He would make them

one thousand times greater. That one thousand dollars was a prophetic sign that something had shifted in my spiritual and financial life. I was experiencing an exodus from the land of lack and an entry into the land of plenty.
God cannot furnish a journey you never embark on. Are you ready to embark on the journey?

Reflection Questions

1. What is the biblical purpose for prosperity? Why is it important?
2. What is meant by the term *fruitfulness*?
3. Why did God give His people the instruction to remember Him?
4. What are the three laws of stewardship? How does this spiritual law relate to prosperity?

Prosperity Prayer

Father, in the name of Jesus, I thank You for who You are and all that You have done in my life. I know that prosperity is not the invention of man, but it is by Your divine purpose that I would prosper in every area of my life. Thank You for demonstrating Your love toward me in the form of Your provision. I declare that lack and insufficiency are not Your will for my life. I declare that I live in the land of plenty and I have more than enough resources to meet the needs of others. I declare that I am a faithful steward of the resources that You have entrusted to my care and that I use these resources for the furthering of Your kingdom in Jesus's name. Amen!

EVEN AS YOUR SOUL PROSPERS

Beloved, I pray that you may prosper in all things and be in health, just as your soul prospers.

—3 John 1:2

Her curiosity was provoked. The subtle yet convincing discourse tantalized her senses. She glanced at the tree again. It was astonishingly beautiful and deeply appealing. *What if I just taste its fruit? What could be the harm in that?* she thought. *After all, it is not like it will kill us!* Little did Eve know that her desire to eat from the Tree of Knowledge of Good and Evil would cost her and her husband peace, provision, and prosperity. To her amazement, one bite of the fruit opened her eyes, not to the bountifulness of the garden of Eden, but to her own depravity and insufficiency. She had been greatly deceived.

Tales from the Garden

What you just read is my own dramatized rendition of the account of the fall in the garden of Eden. You may be wondering why I bring up the garden of Eden once again. The garden is where this all started: the creation of the human race, the mandate given to them by God to be fruitful and multiply, and their ultimate fall from grace.

Earlier, we discussed the purpose and the precedent for biblical prosperity. It took me years to come to the truth that I am now sharing with you in this book. The garden of Eden gives us great insight into God's original design for humanity and mankind's departure from that design. Adam and Eve were in a state of peace before the fall, and that peace was part and parcel of their prosperity. The same is true today. Jesus came to restore that which was forfeited in the garden of Eden.

We said earlier that prosperity is not just financial abundance, but it is indeed fruitfulness in every area of our lives, including our finances. One of the words for prosperity in the Old Testament is the Hebrew word *shalom*, which is used as a salutation but is actually a very complex word. This word is often translated as "peace," but it involves so much more. The word *shalom* means "wholeness or completeness." The idea of this word is "nothing missing and nothing broken," and it also implies the "subduing of or dominion over chaos." It is the wellness of the total man.[1] Adam and Eve lived in perfect shalom before they ate from the Tree of Knowledge of Good and Evil. The moment they ate, their peace was taken away and they entered into spiritual and emotional chaos. They immediately became aware of their own nakedness and insufficiency apart from the presence of God. The condition of their soul was directly connected to their ability to enjoy the abundant life God prepared for them. As mentioned at the beginning of the chapter in 3 John 1:2, the writer of the epistle says, "Beloved, I pray that you may prosper in all things and be in health, just as your soul prospers." In this passage, we can see the correlation between the condition of our soul (the mind, will, and emotions) and our ability to prosper and be in health. Your physical prosperity and health will always be a reflection of the condition of your soul. The condition of your soul affects your ability to walk in abundance. This is why we must understand the necessity of soul prosperity. Jesus didn't die on the cross for you and I to be "broke, busted, and disgusted." He came so that we would enjoy an abundant life in Him (spirit, soul, and body). (See John 10:10.) The only way to experience this abundant life is to embrace it fully.

The Good Shepherd

One of my favorite Psalms is the twenty-third Psalm. Here, King David exclaims, "The LORD is my shepherd; I shall not want. He makes me to lie down in green pastures; He leads me beside the still waters. He restores my soul; He leads me in the paths of righteousness for His name's sake" (Psalm 23:1–3).

As a shepherd, King David understood the role and function of a shepherd, and he makes the poetic analogy

27

that the God of Abraham, Isaac, and Jacob is not just the Shepherd of Israel, but He is his personal Shepherd. It is the responsibility of the Good Shepherd to provide for and protect the sheep. Under the care of this Good Shepherd, the sheep will never lack. Notice that the Shepherd makes His sheep to lie down in green pastures. This represents prosperity and health. The still waters represent peace and tranquility.

Then the writer goes on to say, "He restores my soul . . ." There is an inextricable relationship between the state of the soul and the entirety of the life of the sheep. If the Shepherd only cared for the physical needs of the sheep but neglected their spiritual, mental, and emotional state, He would not be a benevolent Shepherd. But we know that God is good all the time, which is why He is interested in the well-being of our souls. In fact, prosperity flows from the inside out, not the outside in. Too many people are focused on their outward being and have totally neglected the condition of their inward being.

Can you imagine a person filled with bitterness, offense, and resentment and expecting the blessings of God to flow in their life? The soulish life is a mirror reflection of the natural and financial life. When God began teaching me how to prosper, the first area He addressed was my soul. I wasn't whole on the inside. That's right! I could quote Scripture, prophesy, and preach the gospel, but my soul was wounded. I often entertained toxic thoughts and emotions. I was easily offended and often espoused a victim mentality. God had to help me renew my mind before He could repair my money.

Soul Bankruptcy

During my short time on this earth, I have experienced many financial woes. I have been broke, evicted, and homeless. I have had my car repossessed, and at the lowest point in my life, I went into a plasma bank to give plasma so that I could get food. Thankfully, I have never had to file bankruptcy. Typically, this happens when a person can no longer fulfill their debt obligations. This filing takes place in the courts. Bankruptcy can also be defined as the state of being completely lacking in a particular quality or value. Many people may never experience bankruptcy in a legal or financial sense, but they are actually experiencing what I call soul bankruptcy. This means that the person is lacking peace, joy, happiness, etc.

Soul bankruptcy is much worse than financial bankruptcy because the person experiencing this bankruptcy is often unaware of their condition. If left unchecked, this soul bankruptcy can lead to the demise of one's financial life. Just like the financially bankrupt person is weighed down by financial debt, the person experiencing soul bankruptcy is weighed down by spiritual and emotional debt. To clarify, walking in bitterness and resentment is a form of soul bankruptcy. "But he who hates his brother is in darkness and walks in darkness, and does not know where he is going, because the darkness has blinded his eyes" (1 John 2:11).

The Bible says that if we operate in hatred toward our brother or sister (fellow believer), we are in darkness and walking in darkness and don't know where we are going

29

because that darkness has blinded our eyes. This is a very serious verse of Scripture. It is possible to be operating in spiritual darkness as a believer because we are harboring toxic thoughts and emotions toward others. When we harbor these sinful attitudes, we become debt collectors, and in order to be a spiritual debt collector, we must first be in debt ourselves.

The Debt of Unforgiveness

In the Gospel of Matthew, Jesus tells a very powerful story about forgiveness. This parable was sparked by the apostle Peter's question about forgiveness. "Then Peter came to Him and said, 'Lord, how often shall my brother sin against me, and I forgive him? Up to seven times?'" (Matthew 18:21). Jesus's response was both epic and unexpected. "Jesus said to him, 'I do not say to you, up to seven times, but up to seventy times seven'" (Matthew 18:22).

Jesus went further to say this:

> Therefore the kingdom of heaven is like a certain king who wanted to settle accounts with his servants. And when he had begun to settle accounts, one was brought to him who owed him ten thousand talents. But as he was not able to pay, his master commanded that he be sold, with his wife and children and all that he had, and that payment be made. The servant therefore fell down before him, saying, "Master, have patience with me, and I will pay you all." Then the master of that servant was moved with compassion, released him, and forgave him the debt.

30

But that servant went out and found one of his fellow servants who owed him a hundred denarii; and he laid hands on him and took him by the throat, saying, "Pay me what you owe!" So his fellow servant fell down at his feet and begged him, saying, "Have patience with me, and I will pay you all." And he would not, but went and threw him into prison till he should pay the debt. So when his fellow servants saw what had been done, they were very grieved, and came and told their master all that had been done. Then his master, after he had called him, said to him, "You wicked servant! I forgave you all that debt because you begged me. Should you not also have had compassion on your fellow servant, just as I had pity on you?" And his master was angry, and delivered him to the torturers until he should pay all that was due to him.

So My heavenly Father also will do to you if each of you, from his heart, does not forgive his brother his trespasses.

—Matthew 18:23–35

You may have read this account before, but you have probably looked at this story simply from the perspective of forgiving someone who has hurt or disappointed you. A deeper spiritual mystery is found in this parable that every believer must understand in order to walk in biblical prosperity.

We must understand the context of this passage of Scripture. The context is, of course, forgiveness. But we see Jesus use an example about money; the entire parable is about financial debt. There is actually a spiritual correlation between forgiveness and finances. Notice that the servant owes a large debt that he doesn't have the capacity to pay. In a modern sense, this servant would be filing for bankruptcy and facing criminal charges for his debt, yet he actually requests a payment extension from the judge. The judge responds by denying his extension request and instead forgives the debt in total. This is unprecedented. The judge totally wiped away all the servant's debt. The servant does not have to pay one penny ever again.

You would think that he would leave the court with tears of joy and a heart filled with gratitude, yet he responds quite differently. His first course of action is to find his fellow servant, who owed a debt that pales in comparison to the debt he had just been forgiven. He rejected the servant's appeal for an extension (the same appeal that he had just made to the judge) and demanded payment immediately. He went as far as to have his fellow servant thrown in jail for his failure to pay. The judge heard about this, and he summoned the servant and confronted him. He called him a wicked servant because, "I forgave you all that debt . . ." And therein lies the mystery.

The servant received a financial pardon but was still in debt in his soul. Because of his bankruptcy in the soul, he could not let go of the debt his fellow servant owed him. That refusal to let go of the debt in his soul landed him back in financial debt. Many believers are just like this wicked servant in Matthew's account. They harbor unforgiveness, which has landed them in a prison of spiritual debt. They are tormented by tormentors in their minds and emotions. Unlocking this mystery is the key to living an abundant life.

Spiritual Debt and Financial Debt

There is a powerful correlation between spiritual debt and financial debt. Understanding this correlation will give you greater insight as to how to walk in biblical prosperity. First, we need to look at debt and address what it has to do with our spiritual life. *Oxford English Dictionary* defines *debt* as "something, typically money, that is owed or due."[2] Debt is one of the primary sources of poverty in a person's life. This word is derived from the Latin word *debitum*, which means "something owed or to owe."[3]

The servant in Matthew's Gospel account was in debt, and as a result, he and his entire family were in bondage until that debt was forgiven. Spiritual debt is the spiritual and emotional baggage that a person carries in their soul. We were all in debt to sin until Jesus paid the price through His sacrifice that released us from that debt. Although many Christians have been released from their sin debt through the efficacious work of Christ on the cross, they have assumed more spiritual debt through their refusal to release those who have trespassed against them. Just like in nature, the more baggage you carry, the more you are weighed down and stagnant. The more a person harbors spiritual debt, the more the person hinders their ability to prosper in their soul.

God wants you whole in every area of your life, especially your soul (mind, will, and emotions). In the epistle of 3 John 2, the apostle John establishes the correlation between prosperity in the soul and outward prosperity. Every time we address issues in the souls that hinder our ability to appropriate the abundant spiritual life that God has prepared for us in Christ, we are making room for that life to manifest in us physically and financially as well. Simply put, the condition of our souls affects our ability to walk in abundance.

Beloved, a bitter person is a barren person. People would not hold on to bitterness if they knew it would potentially bankrupt them. The first place we need to audit is our thought life. What are you thinking about? What types of thoughts do you entertain? Do you have a positive or negative mental and emotional state?

For years, I walked in bitterness and offense because I didn't realize how detrimental it was to every other area of my life. When someone offended me, I would hold on to that offense for months, even years, at a time. I began to have challenges in my health and in my finances.

At one point, I worked in corporate America. During one of our busy seasons in the insurance industry, I was under a lot of stress and pressure. I became very angry with my coworkers. To be totally honest, I was in a toxic work environment. The senior leadership engaged in a lot of micromanaging and other toxic behaviors. After several weeks, I developed chronic pain, stiffness, and burning in my legs. It resembled the symptoms of gout. I prayed to the Lord and asked Him to heal me.

As I was imploring the Lord's healing one night, He spoke in a still, small voice. "Anger!" I was perplexed! "What was that, Lord?" I replied. He said, "Anger has accumulated in your legs. Release the people, and the pain will leave."

I was shocked, but I knew the Lord was right, so I did as He had instructed. I said, "Lord, I repent for harboring anger toward my coworkers and supervisors. I release them now and forgive them completely." Immediately, I was totally healed. Praise the Lord!

In that moment, I realized the powerful connection between the state of my mind, will, and emotions and my physical health. Could your bitterness toward others be holding up your prosperity? Could your bank account be a reflection of the thoughts you have entertained? A poor soul is a poor bank account. Some of you may be thinking, *But many wealthy people are bitter and angry!* You are absolutely right. Many millionaires and billionaires don't know the Lord and are very wealthy and outwardly prosperous. However, biblical prosperity (as opposed to worldly prosperity) encompasses the whole man (spirit, soul, and body) and not just material wealth. Furthermore, God holds believers to a higher standard than He does the world.

Tales from the Rich Young Ruler

We see a very powerful illustration in the Gospel of Mark concerning the importance of the condition of the soul as it relates to prosperity. The Bible records:

Now as He was going out on the road, one came running, knelt before Him, and asked Him, "Good Teacher, what shall I do that I may inherit eternal life?"

So Jesus said to him, "Why do you call Me good? No one is good but One, that is, God. You know the commandments: 'Do not commit adultery,' 'Do not murder,' 'Do not steal,' 'Do not bear false witness,' 'Do not defraud,' 'Honor your father and your mother.'"

And he answered and said to Him, "Teacher, all these things I have kept from my youth."

Then Jesus, looking at him, loved him, and said to him, "One thing you lack: Go your way, sell whatever you have and give to the poor, and you will have treasure in heaven; and come, take up the cross, and follow Me."

But he was sad at this word, and went away sorrowful, for he had great possessions.

Then Jesus looked around and said to His disciples, "How hard it is for those who have riches to enter the kingdom of God!" And the disciples were astonished at His words. But Jesus answered again and said to them, "Children, how hard it is for those who trust in riches to enter the kingdom of God! It is easier for a camel to go through the eye of a needle than for a rich man to enter the kingdom of God."

And they were greatly astonished, saying among themselves, "Who then can be saved?"

But Jesus looked at them and said, "With men it is impossible, but not with God; for with God all things are possible."

Then Peter began to say to Him, "See, we have left all and followed You."

So Jesus answered and said, "Assuredly, I say to you, there is no one who has left house or brothers or sisters or father or mother or wife or children or lands, for My sake and the gospel's, who shall not receive a hundredfold now in this time—houses and brothers and sisters and mothers and children and lands, with persecutions—and in the age to come, eternal life. But many who are first will be last, and the last first."

—Mark 10:17–31

This is one of the most misunderstood and misquoted Scriptures in the Bible. Many have used this particular passage to justify a certain perspective about wealth and success. But what was Jesus actually saying? Notice that the Bible says a certain ruler came to Jesus asking what he must do to inherit eternal life. Jesus then proceeded to outline the commandments given by Moses, which every devout Jewish man of the time would have observed. The young ruler exclaimed that he had kept all those commandments since he was a child.

Then Jesus told him that he lacked one thing. This is a very important part of the passage because it outlines the key to everything Jesus told this young man. He used the Greek word *leipō* for *lack*, and this word means to "leave behind, or to be destitute or wanting."[4] In other words, Jesus told him that he was destitute or poor. The irony is that this young man was very materially wealthy, yet Jesus said that he was destitute. It doesn't make sense that someone with material wealth was destitute. Jesus told him to sell all that he had and give to the poor and he would have treasure in heaven and that he should come and follow him.

Jesus used an interesting Greek word for *treasure* in this passage, the Greek word *thēsauros*, which means "the place in which good and precious things are collected and laid up or treasury."[5]

This was not a recipe for salvation or eternal life—it was a test. This young man was sorrowful and walked away because in his obsession with material wealth, he rejected the true meaning of prosperity. He built his identity around what he possessed. In reality, his finances were more important than the condition of his soul and his desire to enter the kingdom.

Jesus went on to say, "Assuredly, I say to you that it is hard for a rich man to enter the kingdom of heaven. And again I say to you, it is easier for a camel to go through the eye of a needle than for a rich man to enter the kingdom of God" (Matthew 19:23–24). This is yet another interesting reference. In order to enter the true riches that Jesus is talking about, we must leave our "camel" (i.e., our worldly perception of wealth and riches) behind. Jesus was calling him to let go of his right to his possessions in exchange for greater treasures.

Jesus continued, "Assuredly, I say to you, there is no one who has left house or parents or brothers or wife or children, for the sake of the kingdom of God, who shall not receive many times more in this present time, and in the age to come eternal life" (Luke 18:29–30).

Jesus never said we must be poor to enter the kingdom of God; instead, He actually promised that if we let go of inferior riches, we would receive everything we left behind "in this life" and true riches in the life to come. Hallelujah!

Reflection Questions

1. What pattern does the garden of Eden provide for the relationship between our soul and prosperity?
2. What is the significance of the story of the rich young ruler? How does it relate to believers today?

3. What is spiritual debt? What is the relationship between spiritual debt and financial debt?

4. In the story of the rich young ruler, what did the camel represent? What was Jesus's message to him?

Prosperity Prayer

Father, in the name of Jesus, I declare that You are good and Your mercy endures forever. I know that the devil comes to steal, kill, and destroy, but Your will is that we live an abundant life in Christ. I declare that I will prosper and walk in divine health, even as my soul prospers. My mind, will, and emotions have been restored and renewed by the power of the Holy Spirit. I declare that all spiritual debt in my life has been discharged through the powerful sacrifice of Jesus on the cross and that I no longer live in bondage. I freely forgive all others as I would have You forgive me. I release all those who are indebted to me, and I ask that any lien on my life and destiny, either spiritual or financial, be legally discharged right now in the name of Jesus. Thank You for the abundant life that you have given me. In the name of Jesus. Amen!

Declaration of Abundance

Father, in the name of Jesus, I declare that Your Word is true. Your desire is for me to prosper and be in health even as my soul prospers. I recognize that

You are the source of true prosperity—the shalom that comes from You. This perfect peace means that nothing is missing or broken in my life. My mind is whole. My body is whole. My emotions are whole. I am whole and prosperous in my finances. Thank You, Lord Jesus, for restoring my soul. My soul is prosperous. I refuse to harbor spiritual, emotional, or financial debt of any kind. I freely forgive all those who have trespassed against me, and I freely receive forgiveness for my trespasses. Thank You for Your supernatural abundance in my life and finances in the name of Jesus.

3

POVERTY, THE DESTINY THIEF

So I will restore to you the years that the swarming locust has eaten, the crawling locust, the consuming locust, and the chewing locust, My great army which I sent among you.

—Joel 2:25

As I gazed at his melancholy face, I could not help but wonder how this was possible. How could a boy this young be on the roadside all alone? As I continued to stare, I had so many questions. How old was he? He looked like he was probably about five or six years old. Why wasn't he in school? He stared back at me, emotionless, while he gathered his makeshift brooms made from palm branches. Why couldn't his parents afford school? Why was he selling handmade brooms by the roadside? What if he was meant to be the next minister of health or president? The more I thought about this, the more I began to weep.

The above story is an account of my very first trip to Africa. This young man was selling items by the roadside. As a parent, I could not help but wonder where his parents were. He was all alone, and by the looks of it, he had experience doing what he was doing. At that moment, a light went on. What Adam and Eve did in the garden of Eden didn't just affect the spiritual condition of the human race but opened the door to the spirit of poverty. This poverty was indeed a destiny thief.

I am by no means implying that everyone in Africa is poor. I have been to Africa many times, and there are many wealthy people there. However, many people all over the world are experiencing the debilitating effects of poverty. We said earlier that poverty is not simply a socioeconomic phenomenon but is actually a spiritual power that has entered the earth through sin. It has no regard for race, ethnicity, nationality, gender, or religion. It is the power behind starvation, corruption, human trafficking, and even murder. In my travels around the world, I have witnessed the devastating effects of poverty. Despite this, I am grossly ignorant of the nuances of poverty. The problem of poverty is not solved by solidarity with the poor; it is solved by spiritual and economic empowerment.

Life More Abundantly

In the Gospel of John, Jesus made a very powerful statement. "The thief does not come except to steal, and to kill, and to destroy. I have come that they may have life, and that they may have it more abundantly" (John 10:10). We can clearly see that it is not the will of God that we be destitute and barren.

Jesus said the thief (in reference to false prophets and also the devil) comes to steal. Although the context of this is false prophets who came to manipulate the children of Israel out of their prophetic promises, we can also attribute this same characteristic to the spirit of poverty. That's right! Poverty is a thief and a robber. Poverty is a destiny thief because it inhibits a person from experiencing the abundant life that Jesus paid the price for us to enjoy.

That young man that I saw on the roadside in Africa had been robbed of his future, robbed of his potential, and robbed of his ability to enjoy the basic necessities that many of us enjoy today. This was not some philosophical moment to impose my Western superiority. This was an opportunity to examine myself and my personal ideologies.

I discerned at that moment that poverty was demonic, like cancer spreading through society. Just like physical cancer destroys a person's physical and financial life, the spirit of poverty destroys potential. It is the antithesis to prosperity. Jesus made the contrast. The thief comes to steal, kill, and destroy, but He came to give us life, and that more abundantly. (See John 10:10.) The word for *life* there is the Greek word *zōē*, which means "of the absolute fullness of life, both essential and ethical, which belongs to God, and through him both to the hypostatic 'logos' and to Christ in whom the 'logos' put on human nature" and "life real and genuine, a life active and vigorous, devoted to God, blessed, in the portion even in this world of those who put their trust in Christ, but after the resurrection to be consummated by new accessions (among them a more perfect body), and to last for ever."[1]

This word is a very expressive and comprehensive word that essentially embodies "the life God enjoys." That's right! Jesus came to give us the same life that God Himself enjoys. A conservative seminarian probably just turned over in their grave when I made that statement, but I can assure you that it is absolutely biblical and true.

I had to ask myself, *Was that young boy enjoying the fullness of life? Was he experiencing the vitality of life, full and overflowing?* The answer is obviously no. The only reason any person is not experiencing something that Jesus came to give them is because a thief has stolen it from them.

Identity Theft

Several years ago, I had a very shocking experience. I went to a Mexican restaurant near my house to buy a few tacos for my family. After making the transaction of about twenty-five dollars, I received a notification fifteen minutes later that someone made a purchase in Mexico City for $2,500. What? How was this possible? I had never even been to Mexico. How could I have made a purchase thousands of miles away? The answer is simple; my information was stolen. Someone at that restaurant stole my credit card information and used it to make a fraudulent transaction in my name.

This is called identity theft, which, unfortunately, is a multibillion-dollar business. Every day, millions of people have their identities stolen, and as a result, they are defrauded out of their personal finances and possessions. Whenever there is a theft, the victims lose their ability to enjoy something that belongs to them. Every penny that is stolen is yet another penny that they cannot use. Satan is the greatest identity thief in the world. In fact, his identity theft began in the garden of Eden. He defrauded the human race out of eternal life by convincing them to believe and consume a lie.

Beloved, he is employing the same tactics today. The devil wants people to believe that what they are experiencing is legitimate. He wants people to believe that God wants them poor and broke. He wants people to believe that it is God's will for them to be sick and bitter so that he can rob them of their identity and, in doing so, steal their destiny. The enemy is an illegal entity; therefore, the only way for him to gain access to what belongs to humankind is through deceitful and insidious means. Simply put, he has to steal it to get it. The best way to steal something from a person is to do it without their knowledge. You can't protect something when you don't even know it belongs to you.

As I mentioned before, Adam and Eve were deceived in the garden of Eden. They were convinced to opt for a life and an existence that was inferior to the one God gave them. They settled for the Tree of Knowledge of Good and Evil when, in reality, God gave them access to the Tree of Life. Deception is profound because it essentially involves convincing someone to believe that something is true when it is actually false.

This great deception has been perpetuated for generations. The enemy has been trying to convince people that God is not benevolent. How can you receive from a

God that you don't believe is good? How can you place confidence in a God you believe is good only sometimes? You can't! The problem is that many people, including born-again Christians, believe that God doesn't prosper everyone. They believe that poverty is a part of His will. (We will explore this concept more in a later chapter.)

The record of Scripture is clear. He wants you to have an abundant life. He not only desires the abundant life for you, but He paid the ultimate price (in the form of His very life) for you to receive it. But you will never receive something you don't know is yours. Would that young man that I saw in Africa have accepted his current condition in life if he knew that there was more? Would he have sat by passively if he knew that someone was stealing from him? Can you imagine walking up to him and stealing one of the brooms he spent hours constructing by hand? He would probably yell at you or even chase you down the road, shouting, "Thief!" The fellow market workers would probably join him in apprehending you and, if possible, bring you to justice.

The spirit of poverty is actually a much more malevolent and diabolical thief than enemy human beings could ever be. The theft of your identity and destiny was much more heinous than any theft of your material possessions. It is time to apprehend and prosecute the destiny thief and obtain the life for which Jesus Christ died.

The Spirit of Divine Recompense

We watched him run down the street with a four-hundred-pound piano on his back. I was honestly so impressed by the seemingly supernatural feat of strength that I forgot to focus on the fact that our antique piano had just been stolen. After the awe and wonder subsided, my brother-in-law actually went to the man's house and retrieved the stolen item: our piano.

The previous story is not an exaggeration. This happened to my wife and me in our first year of marriage. We lived in a house in the inner city of Tampa Bay, a community infested with drugs, crime, and prostitution. During our first week in the house, my wife's antique piano that she received as a wedding gift was stolen by a 150-pound drug addict. You heard me correctly! We were truly shocked. Beside the fact that this man should not have been able to carry that piano, we were more amazed that the piano was returned.

We had to confront this thief in order to retrieve what was stolen. Maybe you have never experienced the theft of a piano, but you have experienced the theft of your health, your peace, or your prosperity; you must confront the thief in order to retrieve that which was stolen. Unfortunately for that drug addict and the devil, I am a confrontational person. Fortunately, it has helped me demand the return of what was stolen from me.

If you are reading this, you are about to experience a divine recompense in your life and finances. Just like the thief had to return our antique piano, the enemy of your life must return what he has stolen from you. However, this recompense will not come without a confrontation. The Bible says, "So I will restore to you the years that the swarming locust has eaten, the crawling locust, the consuming locust, and the chewing locust, My great army which I sent among you" (Joel 2:25).

When the Lord began to teach me how to prosper, the first thing that had to change was my mentality. I had to change my perspective on poverty. I had to realize that poverty was not a social condition; it was a demonic spirit, a thief. Most people cannot confront poverty in their life because they are actually a partner with a spirit of poverty. That's right! They are unknowingly (like I was) in agreement with the spirit of poverty. The Bible says, "Whoever is a partner with a thief hates his own life; he swears to tell the truth, but reveals nothing" (Proverbs 29:24).

The Bible says that if we partner with a thief, we actually hate our own soul. This is very powerful. The Bible goes further to say that the person who partners with a thief will hear cursing but will not expose it. The word used here is the Hebrew word *nāḡaḏ*, which means "to be conspicuous, tell, make known or to publish or announce."[2]

Imagine if I would have watched the man steal the piano and not said a word. Granted, I lived in a bad neighborhood at the time, but I still would have been expected to report the crime or file some sort of police report. To neglect to protest the theft would be to consent to the crime. Many people are sitting by while the enemy steals from them. Maybe they are afraid. Maybe they think it's normal. Regardless of the reason, we must change our mindset in order to see a change in our circumstances. God said that He would restore the years that the locusts have eaten.

The word for *restore* there is the Hebrew word *šālam*, which means "to be in the covenant of peace."[3] It is actually a form of the word *shalom*. He says He will restore shalom and wholeness to every area that has been broken, damaged, or wounded. Stop partnering with the thief, and speak out against him. Declare, "Bring back my stuff in the name of Jesus!"

The True Face of Poverty

I want to take a moment and reiterate some of the concepts that we highlighted earlier. Many people are under the impression that poverty is a financial issue. The truth is that most poverty is not financial; it is emotional and spiritual. I will emphasize this very important point throughout this book. Systemic poverty is a real problem. The Presbyterian Mission defines *systemic poverty* as "the economic exploitation of people who are poor through laws, policies, practices and systems that perpetuate their impoverished status."[4] If this definition is true, then it would suggest that poverty is actually an enterprise built upon exploitation.

I am not attempting to go down a rabbit hole of relativism, but I am simply trying to establish that poverty does not always wear the same face. Systemic poverty is connected to those who oppress others emotionally and not just financially. We must see poverty for what it is: oppression. We must also come to recognize the damage that poverty does to individuals and communities and come to actually hate poverty. Again, this is not an anthropological research study, but I am simply trying to establish a baseline understanding that poverty is evil because it is oppression.

The Bible says this about our Lord.

The Spirit of the Lord is upon Me,
Because He has anointed Me
To preach the gospel to the poor;
He has sent Me to heal the brokenhearted,
To proclaim liberty to the captives
And recovery of sight to the blind,
To set at liberty those who are oppressed;
To proclaim the acceptable year of the Lord.

—Luke 4:18–19

Jesus came to set the captives free, but more specifically, He came to preach the gospel to the poor. This is because the poor are the most oppressed group in society. The gospel is the good news. Here is an example of good news for the poor: "Hey, guys, I just want to tell you that you are going to continue in your poverty until you die to bring glory to My name and possibly make it into heaven one day! Sound good?"

That is not what Jesus preached. He actually preached the exact opposite. Every Jew in the first century would have known specifically what Jesus was referring to. They read the scroll of Isaiah often in the synagogue. They knew He was quoting directly from Isaiah 61 and that the particular passage He quoted spoke of the Messiah. The listeners also knew what Jesus meant when He said, "To proclaim [preach] the acceptable year of the Lord."

This was the year of the Jubilee, a time when captives were released, those who owed debt were forgiven, and land was remitted to its original owners. This celebration had very specific financial implications. The only way that the gospel would be good news to the poor was if it announced their jubilee through the Messiah. Jesus came to bring a perpetual jubilee (rest and release) to those who believe in Him. This jubilee doesn't begin when we die but the moment we believe and continues into eternity. We have received our jubilee from sin, bondage, oppression, and poverty through Jesus Christ, our Lord.

Poverty Is Destitution and Oppression

We established earlier that poverty is a consequence of sin. When Adam and Eve fell in the garden of Eden, sin and poverty entered the earth realm. Before sin, there was no such thing as poverty on the planet. The moment poverty entered into the world, mankind began to struggle for their provision and toil in their work. This eventually led to physical death. Adam could not fulfill his assignment on earth. When a person is bound by a spirit of poverty, they are unable to fulfill their assignment. I have said this before and I'll say it again: Poverty is not just a lack of money but extends far beyond money. It is a lack of motivation, initiative, drive, and purpose in life. I am not suggesting that people who are poor are bad. But those bound by poverty are victims of a demonic system built on oppression and exploitation.

The Bible emphatically proclaims what Jesus came to do. "How God anointed Jesus of Nazareth with the Holy Ghost and with power: who went about doing good, and healing all that were oppressed of the devil; for God was with him" (Acts 10:38).

Jesus was anointed with the Holy Spirit, and as a result, He went about doing good and "healing all that were oppressed of the devil." The word *oppression* here comes from the Greek word *katadynasteuō*, which means "to exercise harsh control over one, to use one's power against one."[5] It comes from the Greek root word *dynastēs*, which means "a prince, a potentate, or authority."[6]

As you can probably see from the similarities, we get the word *dynasty* from this root. Google Dictionary defines a *dynasty* as "a line of hereditary rulers of a country."[7] In other words, Jesus came to liberate people from the control or power of "harsh princes" or "authorities" that are hereditary and generational. Poverty is an oppressive authority or principality that actually controls people, cultures, and nations. Jesus came to set the captives free from their captivity. We are no longer slaves to the demonic dynasty of poverty and oppression.

The Anointing Destroys the Yoke of Poverty

At one time, I was bound by a spirit of poverty. Years ago, I was in such a dark place that I had to go to a plasma bank to give plasma (not blood) to get food for my family. This is not to vilify anyone who has taken a similar course of action, but I am highlighting my personal journey. I remember this as if it were last night. My wife was actually pregnant at the time, and I didn't know what to do, so I told her that I was going to stop by the plasma bank on the way home. She waited in the car while I went inside. The building had a specific unpleasant odor. Questionable individuals occupied the waiting room.

As I was filling out the medical forms and liability waiver, I looked around the room, and the entire place became silent. It was as if someone pushed the mute button. As I pondered the silence, the audible voice of God spoke. "Kynan, what are you doing here?" Before I could answer, He spoke again. "This is *not* your portion!" I tore out of the building. When I entered the car, my wife asked me what happened. I told her that I couldn't do it. "God told me no!" I was embarrassed. I was frustrated. I was perplexed. I don't remember how we ate that night, but I know that God provided somehow. I will never forget that night.

My financial state at that time not only affected me but affected my wife and my unborn child. If my wife was malnourished because of the lack of money, my baby was also malnourished. Since I was not walking in my purpose at that time, my wife and baby weren't realizing their purpose either. The more I thought about it, the more I realized the profound effect of my thoughts and decisions on everyone connected to me.

As difficult as it is to reflect on such a challenging season in our lives, in that moment, everything changed in my life. After this experience, I had a supernatural encounter with the Lord. The Spirit of the Lord came upon me and said, "Son, I have given you an anointing for financial deliverance. I have raised you to be a financial deliverer in the body of Christ." At the time the Lord spoke to me, I couldn't even afford to pay attention. What did He mean by "financial deliverer"? Now, I finally understand what the Lord was saying to me years ago.

As we mentioned before, poverty is not simply a socioeconomic condition, but the spirit of poverty enslaves people to a worldview that is antithetical to the kingdom of God. Poverty affects national destinies and communities. We will not be able to rid the world of poverty (because of the effects of sin) until Jesus returns, but we do not have to accept poverty as a normal way of life, no more than we accept addiction, abuse, or depression as a normal way of life. We must contend for the abundant life that God has graciously provided for us in Christ. God has called me and so many others in the body of Christ to raise a standard. We have been anointed to destroy the yoke of poverty in our families and communities. Using finances, we have been empowered to tangibly advance the kingdom of God.

Reflection Questions

1. What are the effects of poverty on families, communities, and nations?
2. Why is poverty referred to as a destiny thief? What is the correlation between prosperity and destiny?
3. What are the emotional effects of systemic poverty? How do people break free?
4. What does it mean to be a financial deliverer for the body of Christ?

Prosperity Prayer

Lord, I thank You that You have delivered me from the thief called poverty who seeks to steal my destiny.

I renounce every lie of the devil that suggests that it is Your will for me to be poor and live in misery. I recognize that poverty is the consequence of the curse that came in through sin, and therefore, I have been redeemed from the curse of poverty in the name of Jesus. Just as it is not Your will for me to live in sin, it is not Your will for me to be a slave to the poverty system instituted by Satan. I take authority over the spirit of deception that seeks to keep me and my bloodline in bondage to a life of struggle and defeat. Thank You for breaking this curse off me and for Your loving-kindness in my life, in the name of Jesus. Amen!

THE JOSEPH MANDATE

And the LORD was with Joseph, and he was a prosperous man; and he was in the house of his master the Egyptian.

—Genesis 39:2 KJV

His eyes were filled with tears as he hid behind the wall, trying his best to stay unnoticed. After all these years, he had finally been reunited with his brothers. Yet they did not even recognize him. His heart pounded as he reflected on his perilous journey to the palace. He was betrayed, abandoned, enslaved, falsely accused, and imprisoned. Now, here he stood, the vice-regent of the most powerful kingdom in the known world. He had become a father to Pharaoh, and his dream from so long ago had finally come to pass.

Joseph

One of my favorite stories in the Bible is the story of Joseph in Genesis 39. We know that Joseph dreamed a dream and shared it with his father and older brothers and was ultimately thrown into a pit and sold into slavery as a result. Talk about a bad day! But the story of Joseph is not just another story of tragedy and triumph but is actually a prophetic blueprint for the church in the end times. First of all, we must look at Joseph's name as a clue into the significance of this biblical narrative. In the Bible, we know that names are very important. The name Joseph (*yôsēp̄* in Hebrew) means "Jehovah has added."[1] This gives us a deeper insight into what the story of Joseph represents. This is a story of *increase*, a story of God's prosperity.

Essentially, Joseph is the son of Jacob (Israel) who was sent into Egypt by the sovereign hand of Jehovah. Initially, it seems like a very sad and tragic tale, but at the end, it turns out to be very powerful and providential. The Bible records:

> And Pharaoh said to his servants, "Can we find such a one as this, a man in whom is the Spirit of God?"
>
> Then Pharaoh said to Joseph, "Inasmuch as God has shown you all this, there is no one as discerning and wise as you. You shall be over my house, and all my people shall be ruled according to your word; only in regard to the throne will I be greater than you." And Pharaoh said to Joseph, "See, I have set you over all the land of Egypt."
>
> Then Pharaoh took his signet ring off his hand and put it on Joseph's hand; and he clothed him in garments of

fine linen and put a gold chain around his neck. And he had him ride in the second chariot which he had; and they cried out before him, "Bow the knee!" So he set him over all the land of Egypt. Pharaoh also said to Joseph, "I am Pharaoh, and without your consent no man may lift his hand or foot in all the land of Egypt." And Pharaoh called Joseph's name Zaphnath-Paaneah. And he gave him as a wife Asenath, the daughter of Poti-Pherah priest of On. So Joseph went out over all the land of Egypt.

Joseph was thirty years old when he stood before Pharaoh king of Egypt. And Joseph went out from the presence of Pharaoh, and went throughout all the land of Egypt.

—Genesis 41:38–46

To paraphrase this powerful account, Joseph was elevated into the highest position in the land beside Pharaoh and put in charge of the economic well-being of the entire kingdom of Egypt. No man could lift up their hand or their foot in the entire nation without his permission. This is amazing! A former felon became the vice-regent of the most powerful empire of its time. Notice the question that Pharaoh asked his servants, "Who can find a man such as this, a man in whom the Spirit of God is?" Joseph was not praised for his ability to make sacrifices in the temple or even for his dreams. He was praised for his ability to operate in the wisdom of God. There is a correlation between the wisdom of God and prosperity.

God is raising up a generation of believers who will operate in supernatural wisdom. They will carry the Spirit of God. This supernatural wisdom was not for the religious mountain; it was for the economy. In addition, Joseph was not known in the land for his dreams. This is actually a common misconception. Joseph only had one dream recorded in Scripture: his dream that his father and brothers bowed to him. However, the gifting and ability that is most highlighted in the scriptural account of Joseph is his ability to administer and manage resources.

You Must Manage before It Manifests

As I mentioned at the beginning of the chapter, the Bible records, "And the LORD was with Joseph, and he was a prosperous man; and he was in the house of his master the Egyptian" (Genesis 39:2 KJV). Joseph was said to be a prosperous man. But there is an issue with the timing of this statement. In Genesis 39, Joseph was enslaved and taken into Potiphar's house. The Bible doesn't say that Joseph was going to be a prosperous man in the future; it says he was a prosperous man.

He was a slave with no material possessions, yet the Bible calls him prosperous. This begs the question of what the biblical definition of *prosperity* really is. Though Joseph had no physical wealth at the time, he possessed the spirit of prosperity. What is the spirit of prosperity? Joseph had an awareness of the overwhelming and abiding presence of God. This is the same as when God spoke to me years ago and told me that I had an anointing for financial deliverance even though I had no money in my bank account. The shalom of God rested upon Joseph, which was the secret to his prosperity. Everywhere he went, the Lord was with him, and he operated in a spirit of excellence.

He was being developed into a financial deliverer from the very beginning of his journey with God.

Many people today are looking at their lack of resources or limitations, and they don't realize that because the Lord is with them, they are actually prosperous, and it is only a matter of time before that prosperity manifests materially.

Oftentimes, when we read the Scriptures, we don't realize the duration of time that has elapsed between passages. Joseph was about thirteen when he was initially sold into slavery and thirty by the time he came into power. Do the math: seventeen years of slavery and bondage. That is a very long time. The consistent factor during all those years of captivity was Joseph's ability to manage resources of people and materials. We stated earlier that the dominant gift that Joseph exemplified was his management ability. This is what the Word of God says in Genesis 39:

> Now Joseph had been taken down to Egypt. And Potiphar, an officer of Pharaoh, captain of the guard, an Egyptian, bought him from the Ishmaelites who had taken him down there. The LORD was with Joseph, and he was a successful man; and he was in the house of his master the Egyptian. And his master saw that the LORD was with him and that the LORD made all he did to prosper in his hand. So Joseph found favor in his sight, and served him. Then he made him overseer of his house, and all that he had he put under his authority. So it was, from the time that he had made him overseer of his house and all that he had, that the LORD blessed the Egyptian's house for Joseph's sake; and the blessing of the LORD was on all that he had in the house and in the field. Thus he

left all that he had in Joseph's hand, and he did not know what he had except for the bread which he ate.

—Genesis 39:1–6

The first thing we see is that Potiphar (his Egyptian master) recognizes that the Lord was with him because all that he did prospered in his hand. We must discuss this very important point. It does not say that Potiphar knew that God was with him because of his prophetic words or his prayer life. There is only one sign associated with the Lord being with Joseph: stewardship. The works of Joseph's hands testified that the Lord was with him.

The ungodly and unbelieving are not moved by our profession of faith; they are moved by what we do in the name of the Lord. Are you like Joseph? Can people recognize that God is with you by the quality of your work? Joseph never complained. He never cursed Potiphar. He allowed the spirit of prosperity to flow through his life and transform the environment around him. In fact, he was such an excellent manager and steward that Potiphar made him the overseer of his entire estate. (See Genesis 39:5.)

This is a powerful spiritual principle: You must manage before it manifests. God wants to see that you are properly stewarding your measure of influence before He trusts you with more. The key to biblical prosperity is not asking for more; it is stewarding what you already have so that you can be given more. Why would God give you a new car and you don't maintain the car you currently have? Why would God give you a new house when you cannot keep your current house clean? These spiritual mysteries will enable us to unlock greater manifestations of prosperity in our lives.

The Three Josephs: A Prophetic Prototype for the Church

The story of Joseph's life and journey in Egypt is not just a story of Joseph but is an archetype for the church. The church is now entering its finest and most critical hour. In fact, we are living in one of the most important times in human history. History tends to repeat itself, but thankfully, God has a prophetic pattern that He always outlines to prepare us for what is to come. There is a current Joseph mandate. God is preparing and equipping a generation to usher in one of the most glorious times in the history of the world. We call this the Joseph mandate because the pattern of the three Josephs is coming to the forefront of kingdom economics once again.

I want to take a moment and talk about the three Josephs in Scripture. Although more than three people in the Bible were named Joseph, I want to focus on these three because of their spiritual significance as it relates to biblical prosperity. We have already begun to discuss Joseph, the son of Jacob, but let's reiterate and summarize a few more elements about his life.

Joseph, Son of Jacob

We know that Joseph was a son of Jacob (renamed Israel), was rejected by his brothers, and was sold into slavery in Egypt. At the time, Egypt was the economic and spiritual center of the world. He went from the pit to Potiphar's house to the palace. But this is not simply about Joseph's journey; it is about the purpose of this journey, which Scripture highlights in Genesis 45.

> And Joseph said to his brothers, "Please come near to me." So they came near. Then he said: "I am Joseph your brother, whom you sold into Egypt. But now, do not therefore be grieved or angry with yourselves because you sold me here; for God sent me before you to preserve life."
>
> —Genesis 45:4–5

Joseph was promoted to address the impending famine during his lifetime. There were seven years of plenty and seven years of famine. However, in Genesis 45, Joseph reveals the real purpose for his promotion and prosperity. "For God did send me before you to preserve life." Glory to God! Joseph was sent as an emissary and empowered to prosper in order to bring financial preservation and deliverance to an entire nation. If Israel and the patriarchs of the twelve tribes perished in the famine, Joseph, the father of Jesus, would have never been born. This is very powerful. God raised up one man to preserve an entire generation. This should help us understand that prosperity is not just for the individual. Biblical prosperity affects generations.

Joseph, the Father of Jesus

The next example we should consider when exploring this Joseph mandate is Joseph, the father of Jesus. We see some very interesting parallels with Joseph, the son of Jacob. Obviously, they have the same name ("Jehovah has added"), but he is the father of the Messiah, Jesus ("Jehovah is salvation").[2] The correlation in their names alone is actually a prophetic statement: Jehovah has added, Jehovah saves. By combining these two names, we see that Jehovah adds to bring salvation. Glory to God! This is the entire summation of biblical prosperity: God prospers His people to deliver them.

> Now when they had departed, behold, an angel of the Lord appeared to Joseph in a dream, saying, "Arise, take the young Child and His mother, flee to Egypt, and stay there until I bring you word; for Herod will seek the young Child to destroy Him."
>
> —Matthew 2:13

Yet again, God raised up Joseph and called him to go down to Egypt by divine providence in order to preserve the life of Jesus. In other words, the body of Christ was protected from premature demise. If Herod killed Jesus before His time, the plan of redemption could not be fulfilled. Joseph had to be sensitive and obedient to the Spirit of God in order to strategically navigate the perils of his time. Look at what the Bible says:

> Now when Herod was dead, behold, an angel of the Lord appeared in a dream to Joseph in Egypt, saying, "Arise, take the young Child and His mother, and go to the land of Israel, for those who sought the young Child's life are dead." Then he arose, took the young Child and His mother, and came into the land of Israel.
>
> —Matthew 2:19–21

Joseph kept Jesus in Egypt during a season of hazard and danger, and once that season was fulfilled and those who sought the young child's harm perished, God released Joseph to go back into the land of Israel. We see Joseph, Egypt, and Israel once again. Pay attention to this pattern: God raised up a person to preserve His remnant during perilous times and thereby facilitate generational salvation. So like Joseph of Egypt, Joseph of Jesus is not a rabbi, a teacher, or a religious leader; he is actually an entrepreneur. God used an entrepreneur who was sensitive to His voice to preserve the body of Christ. What if God was looking for successful men and women whom He could partner with to preserve the body of Christ in these financially perilous times? What if you were the person God wanted to prosper so that He could usher in revival that would transform the landscape of the world?

Joseph of Arimathea

We have seen the pattern of the two Josephs in the Bible whom God used to preserve His people, but there is yet another prophetic prototype in the form of Joseph of Arimathea. Who is Joseph of Arimathea? The Bible says this:

> After this, Joseph of Arimathea, being a disciple of Jesus, but secretly, for fear of the Jews, asked Pilate that he might take away the body of Jesus; and Pilate gave him permission. So he came and took the body of Jesus.
>
> —John 19:38

We don't know much about Joseph except the fact that he is from a place called Arimathea. He appears in all three

Synoptic Gospels. The most detailed account of Joseph of Arimathea is found in Matthew's Gospel:

> Now when evening had come, there came a rich man from Arimathea, named Joseph, who himself had also become a disciple of Jesus. This man went to Pilate and asked for the body of Jesus. Then Pilate commanded the body to be given to him. When Joseph had taken the body, he wrapped it in a clean linen cloth, and laid it in his new tomb which he had hewn out of the rock; and he rolled a large stone against the door of the tomb, and departed.
>
> —Matthew 27:57–60

The Bible says that he was a rich man, a disciple of Jesus. Mark's account records that he was a counselor. Joseph used his means and his status to compel Pilate to release the body of Jesus and have it delivered to himself. Then Joseph wrapped His body in clean linen and placed Him in a brand-new tomb. Here, we see that God uses another Joseph to preserve the physical body of Jesus until His resurrection. If Jesus's body had been destroyed prematurely, it wouldn't have been available for a physical resurrection.

We know that God is all-powerful, and maybe He could have used another means to raise His Son from the dead, but to flow within natural order, a resurrection needs a body. Interestingly, God didn't use one of the twelve apostles to negotiate the delivery of the body of Jesus, but He used a secret disciple who happened to be a wealthy counselor to preserve the body of His Son. The word

Arimathea means "heights."[3] This is significant. God used a man at the height of society and commerce to affect the future generations. Unfortunately, many have a wrong view of the Word of God and assert that people must be preachers and pastors to be effective in the kingdom.

Where are the Josephs? Where are those who will prosper and use their prosperity to transform culture? Why is all this so important? God has called every one of us as a Joseph to use our resources to tangibly impact the body of Christ and the world. We are the body of Christ and need to be preserved spiritually, physically, and financially until the second coming of Jesus. God is looking for a people who will prosper and use their resources to expand His kingdom.

The Paradigm Shift

The church must experience a paradigm shift. Later, we will discuss God's will to prosper His people in the end times and the great transfer of wealth, but for now, we need to pay close attention to the biblical pattern. In all three examples of Joseph, God worked in partnership with His people to establish heaven's agenda on earth. We can only imagine what would have happened if Joseph wasn't sold into slavery, if he didn't manage well, if he didn't walk in integrity, and if he didn't interpret Pharaoh's dream correctly. We probably would be reading a totally different story in the Bible. The idea that events just happen through osmosis (without the active participation of human beings) is theologically lazy. It is time to believe in your heart and with all your might that God desires to prosper you in every area of your life so that you can be engaged in propagating His divine agenda on earth.

Reflection Questions

1. What is the Joseph mandate, and why is it important in the end times?
2. What is the biblical pattern of the three Josephs in the Bible? How do they establish a blueprint for prosperity in the earth?
3. What is meant by the spirit of prosperity, and how do we operate in it?
4. How important is it to manage the resources God has given us?

Prosperity Prayer

Father, in the name of Jesus, I thank You for who You are and all that You have done in my life. Right now, I receive the anointing for financial deliverance that was upon Joseph of Egypt—I declare that I am a financial deliverer in my generation and that I will use the grace given to me to help people come out of slavery to poverty. Thank You for your supernatural wisdom and witty inventions that will be utilized to bring financial increase to the body of Christ. I surrender my gifts, talents, and abilities to You, Lord, and I ask that You would use them for Your glory.

Let my life be a visible example of Your grace and goodness. Demonstrate Your supernatural provision and divine prosperity through me that others may know and experience Your benevolence in their lives. I receive and walk in Your divine mandate to disciple the nations in Jesus's name. Amen!

5

REAL VERSUS FALSE PROSPERITY

Behold, these are the ungodly, who prosper in the world;
they increase in riches.

—Psalm 73:12 KJV

We see many people in the world—billionaires, celebrities,
leaders of industries—who don't pray or love God, yet
they are wealthy. Christians often ask me questions about
why this is. It is a sort of circular reasoning that seeks to
invalidate biblical prosperity. They suggest that we don't
need biblical prosperity, because people who are unbeliev-
ers are already successful without God. (I will deal with
these issues more extensively in a later chapter.) However,
we must understand the difference between what I call real
prosperity and what I call fake prosperity.

In this chapter, I will focus on making the distinction between the two types of prosperity. Why is this so vital? Millions of Christians are rejecting prosperity as a whole because they have conflated real with fake prosperity.

More Money, More Problems

Oftentimes, when we use the word *prosperity*, it tends to create an image in a person's head, especially when a preacher uses it or when it is used to describe a preacher. The first image that this word brings to mind might be a wealthy banker, a real-estate mogul, a famous rapper, a professional athlete, or even a rich televangelist standing in front of his multimillion-dollar mansion and private jet. Perhaps the word *prosperity* negatively triggers you. Nonetheless, we must reckon with this word because, as I mentioned before, this was not the invention of a televangelist or business man; it was indeed the plan of God to prosper His people.

Years ago, a popular rap song came out called "Mo Money Mo Problems." I won't get into the lyrics of this song, but suffice it to say that the song describes the perils and pitfalls of financial wealth. But biblical prosperity follows a totally different set of rules than fake prosperity. The Bible says, "The blessing of the LORD makes one rich, and He adds no sorrow with it" (Proverbs 10:22). Yes, according to God's Word, you can be prosperous and have joy. You can have material wealth and be generous. Money does not have to mean more problems in your life. How would these mindset changes affect the way you see abundance? The truth is, money is a magnifier. It amplifies and magnifies what is already present in a person's life. The truth is, "Mo Money Mo whatever is already in you!"

Money Is an Instrument

Imagine a fictional court case: Jane Doe vs. Random Kitchen Knife Co. In this case, the plaintiff, Jane Doe, is suing the defendant, Random Kitchen Knife Co., for punitive damages. She claims that if no kitchen knives were manufactured, then she would not have stabbed her ex-husband eighty times. A case like this should immediately be thrown out, but in the highly litigious and deeply unaccountable society we live in today, I am not quite sure what would happen.

The point is, however, that many Christians are making a similar claim about money. Just because someone misuses something doesn't make the thing itself inherently bad or evil. The same knife that Jane Doe used to stab her husband is probably the same knife she used to make chicken pot pie or cut his birthday cake, etc. Beloved, money is an instrument that can be used for good or evil, righteousness or unrighteousness. We have used our resources as a ministry to feed the homeless, rescue women from sex trafficking, provide the basic necessities of those in need, and the list goes on.

It is absurd to believe because a person has a large inventory of kitchen knives that they may be more tempted to become a serial killer. Biblical prosperity has the ability to transform people's lives and demonstrate the unconditional love of God.

Exposing Counterfeit Prosperity

The term *prosperity gospel* refers to the so-called health-and-wealth message that became popular in the early nineties and beyond. This term has taken on a very negative connotation within Christian evangelicalism. But actually, there is no such thing as the prosperity gospel. The term *prosperity gospel* was neither created nor coined by its alleged adherents but popularized by its detractors. Ironically, many of these so-called detractors of the prosperity gospel are very prosperous themselves. In fact, some detractors of the prosperity-gospel message are even millionaires and quite wealthy themselves. Wow! Talk about a theological conundrum!

I'll say this again: There is no such thing as a prosperity gospel; there is only the gospel. Either someone is preaching the true gospel or a false gospel. Within the gospel is the message of prosperity, healing, deliverance, reconciliation, brotherly love, etc. We don't often hear people say that a person is preaching the brotherly love gospel or the deliverance gospel. Prosperity seems to be the only aspect that is singled out. I firmly believe that the devil hates biblical prosperity because the fruitfulness and multiplication and replenishing of the earth by mankind is yet another reminder to the devil that he was kicked out of heaven and that he will soon face eternal damnation and destruction.

As the god of this world, the enemy seeks to keep God's people in spiritual, mental, physical, and financial bondage. If the body of Christ came to a true understanding and revelation of biblical prosperity, it would threaten the well-being of his kingdom. This is why the enemy promotes a counterfeit prosperity. This is a prosperity that is only focused on material possessions and greed. It is the pursuit of wealth for personal consumption and not for the glory of God. Counterfeit prosperity destroys while biblical prosperity builds.

Below, we have a comparison-and-contrast chart between biblical prosperity and false prosperity.

Biblical Prosperity	False Prosperity
establishes God's kingdom, God's agenda	establishes man's kingdom/agenda
benefits others	benefits self
about giving	about accumulating/taking
driven by love	driven by lust
establishes dignity, e.g., when Jesus fed the multitudes, he gave people dignity, people felt the love of God	removes dignity, e.g., OnlyFans site, objectifies people, the person exists for the benefit of others • example: when I was at my worst financially, you have to lose dignity to receive help/benefit (LBJ movement with welfare system with no child's father living with the woman) • you have to do something that compromises integrity
having everything you need to do everything you're called to do	having everything you want to do anything you want to do

What Does Real Wealth Look Like?

We have established that there is a difference between real and false prosperity. The question remains: What does real wealth look like? Growing up, I watched a television show called *Lifestyles of the Rich and Famous*, a documentary-style show that highlighted the opulence of ultra-wealthy individuals. It focused on mansions, exotic cars, yachts, private jets, and other accoutrements. I thought this was the totality of wealth.

I was under the impression that wealth was simply the accumulation of expensive material possessions by people who thought they were better than others. A man wearing an ascot and holding a pipe often came to mind when I heard the word *wealth*. What does real wealth look like? As I have stated before, biblical prosperity means having everything that we need to do everything we have been called to do and more.

The Bible gives us some insight into God's definition of wealth. Biblical wealth is

- leaving an inheritance to your children.
- financing the kingdom of God.
- radical faith, obedience, and giving.
- not being a slave to an ungodly system (Israel was the lender, not the borrower).
- not being a slave to debt.

Let's take a look at some of these.

1. Leaving an Inheritance to Your Children's Children

The Bible is very clear that the power to obtain wealth comes from God (see Deuteronomy 8:18). Proverbs (the Book of Wisdom) tells us more about the purpose of wealth: "A good man leaves an inheritance to his children's children, but the wealth of the sinner is stored up for the righteous" (Proverbs 13:22).

The Bible says a good man leaves an inheritance to his grandchildren. But one can't leave an inheritance to their grandchildren if they are barely getting by. We said before that one of the most selfish things that a person can do is refuse to prosper. That's because a refusal to walk in the prosperity of God (both spiritually and materially) is to make the statement, through your actions if not your words, that the next generation is irrelevant.

If a good man leaves an inheritance, then the wicked man must do the opposite. Instead of an inheritance, he leaves debt. He leaves financial hardship. He leaves the struggle. You must decide whether you will be a good man or woman, or a wicked man or woman. Those who are operating in counterfeit prosperity are simply storing up wealth for those who will be generous in the kingdom of God. Do you want to be among those who receive the wealth of the wicked?

2. Financing the Kingdom of God

In the example of the three Josephs and the Joseph mandate, we can see that God's agenda is to raise up people who will finance the kingdom of God in a very pragmatic sense. This is important because whoever controls the wealth controls the narrative. This does not mean that we must somehow do away with the wealth of the world. That would be ridiculous. However, it does mean that God desires to promote His children into places of influence in the marketplace so that we can begin to impact the decisions that affect the church. Remember, "And you

shall remember the Lord your God, for it is He who gives
you power to get wealth, that He may establish His covenant which He swore to your fathers, as it is this day"
(Deuteronomy 8:18).

God wants to empower the church with the supernatural ability to obtain wealth in order to establish His
covenant. The Hebrew word for *establish* in that verse is
qûm, which means "to arise or stand up."[1] Hallelujah! God
wants to empower us to stand up, not just spiritually but
financially as well. He desires for His agenda to rise up
in the earth. Imagine building churches instead of strip
clubs. Think about funding a young girl's education and
spiritual development instead of her sale into slavery by
a human trafficker. How many lives could be changed for
the glory of God? Both good and evil require finances to
operate on the earth. Which one do you choose?

3. Radical Faith, Radical Obedience, and Radical Giving
　　Back in 2019, the Lord spoke to me before the so-called
pandemic spread all over the world. He told me to begin
teaching the church about the kingdom economy of God.
During that time, God said that there would be a shift in
global economics. I was not sure what God was talking
about. Nonetheless, I said what He told me to say. As I
began to do more research, I came to discover that a great
economic reset was on the horizon. The Babylonian system of finance was beginning to fail. He told me to teach
His people how to prosper in perilous times. The Lord
gave me three distinct keys: radical faith, radical obedience, and radical giving.

The Bible says, "Now faith is the substance of things hoped for, the evidence of things not seen" (Hebrews 11:1). There is an inextricable correlation between biblical faith and biblical prosperity. Unfortunately, many American Christians have learned more intellectualism and psychobabble than they have faith.

Many Christians seem to be operating in growing cynicism. As a pastor, I have often heard the conversations of thousands of Christians to my own shock and awe. "I just don't know how I am going to make it through!," or "I am going through a really hard time!" Where is the faith in that? Instead, people should say, "I know God is in control!," or "I place my confidence in the Word of God despite my circumstances." Faith is the key to unlocking the supernatural power of God. Faith is also the key to unlocking God's unlimited provision for your life. The Spirit of the Lord spoke to me. "You must walk in radical faith to see supernatural results." God is calling us to operate in radical faith; we must believe the impossible, see the invisible, and receive the intangible.

The second thing the Lord told me would be required in this season is radical obedience. In John 2, we see a great example of radical obedience. While at a wedding, the host ran out of wine. Mary, the mother of Jesus, knew that she needed to respond accordingly to see the miracle come to fruition. When she came to Jesus, asking Him to intervene in the current crisis the people found themselves in, He responded, "Woman, what does your concern have to do with Me? My hour has not yet come" (John 2:4). She said to the servants, "Whatever He says to you, do it" (John 2:5).

It almost reminds you of a particular sports apparel slogan. "Just do it!" We must be willing to do whatever He says and obey any and every instruction that Jesus gives us. Beloved, this is the key to unlocking biblical prosperity. We can see what happened in the end: The water became wine.

At one time, God told my wife and I to go to South Tampa (a high-end community) to plant our church when we had no money and no denominational backing. "God, did I hear You correctly?" We were definitely hearing from God even though it did not seem like it at first. At times, we questioned our decisions. The church was not growing. Money seemed to run out. Regardless of the circumstances, we kept obeying the still, small voice of God. Eventually, our radical obedience yielded tremendous fruit. God is calling every one of His children to walk in radical obedience.

According to an article from CDF Capital, 5 percent of Christians in the United States tithe.[2] According to another article by the Christian Post, only 13 percent of evangelicals in the United States tithe.[3] Another study done by Barna Group published in 2022 claims that two out of five Christians in the US tithe to a local church.[4]

Jesus was very clear: "For where your treasure is, there will your heart be also" (Matthew 6:21). Based on the words of Jesus, American Christians do not seem to treasure the kingdom of God. What you value is indicated by what you invest in. But so many Christians claim to love Jesus while giving Him as little as possible. If these studies are true, it reveals a disturbing mindset in the body of Christ. This would also explain why so many are not enjoying the life that Jesus paid such a great price for us to receive. Generosity is part and parcel of the Christian life. (We will talk more about the law of seedtime and harvest in a later chapter.)

If we are going to experience supernatural provision and live an abundant life, we must embrace a lifestyle of radical giving. In my understanding, giving radically is giving sacrificially. I am reminded of the widow who gave all that she had. Jesus declared that she gave more than anyone else because her giving cost her!

Years ago, in one of the darkest times in my spiritual life, the Lord spoke to me and told me to give four thousand dollars, which was all the money I had at the time. At first, I questioned whether I was really hearing the voice of God; then I quickly conceded and obeyed. Remember, it requires radical faith to engage in radical obedience, and it requires radical obedience to give radically. Whatever He says, just do it! Once you learn to live this way, you posture your life for continual miracles, signs, and wonders.

A powerful story of radical giving is found in 1 Kings 17.

Then the word of the Lord came to him, saying, "Arise, go to Zarephath, which belongs to Sidon, and dwell there. See, I have commanded a widow there to provide for you." So he arose and went to Zarephath. And when he came to the gate of the city, indeed a widow was there gathering sticks. And he called to her and said, "Please bring me a little water in a cup, that I may drink." And as she was going to get it, he called to her and said, "Please bring me a morsel of bread in your hand."

So she said, "As the Lord your God lives, I do not have bread, only a handful of flour in a bin, and a little oil in a jar; and see, I am gathering a couple of sticks that I may go in and prepare it for myself and my son, that we may eat it, and die."

And Elijah said to her, "Do not fear; go and do as you have said, but make me a small cake from it first, and bring it to me; and afterward make some for yourself and your son. For thus says the Lord God of Israel: 'The bin of flour shall not be used up, nor shall the jar of oil run dry, until the day the Lord sends rain on the earth.' "

So she went away and did according to the word of Elijah; and she and he and her household ate for many days. The bin of flour was not used up, nor did the jar of oil run dry, according to the word of the Lord which He spoke by Elijah.

—1 Kings 17:8–16

The prophet Elijah was sent to a poor woman of Zarephath who God said would sustain him. When the woman tells Elijah that she just has enough food for her and her son to eat and die, he responds by saying, "Great, go ahead and do that, but feed me first." Yes, you read that correctly! He tells a poor woman to feed him first before feeding her starving child.

Imagine this was in the present day and the preacher showed up to a poor woman's house and asked her to feed him before she feeds her dying children. If that happened today, the news media would probably show up on the scene shortly thereafter to report the latest scandal of spiritual and financial abuse in the church. This would

81

probably end up on a *60 Minutes* or *TMZ* special. Yet that is exactly what Elijah told her to do. In fact, he prophesied to her that if she would obey his instruction, her oil and meal would never run out. Glory to God!

Her radical giving facilitated a miracle of miraculous provision. I believe that God is performing the same miracles today. Will you trust Him despite the limits in your financial resources? Will you operate in radical obedience? Heaven is waiting on your radical faith, radical obedience, and radical giving today.

Reflection Questions

1. How does the amount of money we have access to affect how many problems we have?
2. What does real wealth look like?
3. What are the three distinct keys to prospering in perilous times?
4. How will God raise up people in the last days to finance the kingdom of God in the earth?

Prosperity Prayer

Father, in the name of Jesus, I recognize that You are the only legitimate source of prosperity and any other source of prosperity outside of Your will is counterfeit prosperity. Thank You, Father, that You are the One who gives us the power to get wealth in order that we may establish Your covenant in the earth, according to Deuteronomy 8:18. I recognize that real wealth is not just about the accumulation of material possessions but the advancement of Your kingdom. I declare that I have the power to get wealth, and I will use this wealth to further Your kingdom and agenda in the earth. I declare that I possess radical faith and radical obedience, and I am a radical giver in the name of Jesus. I declare that I will prosper in perilous times because of the power of Your Word in the name of Jesus. Amen!

6

THE POWER OF THE BLESSING

Blessed be the God and Father of our Lord Jesus Christ,
who has blessed us with every spiritual blessing in the
heavenly places in Christ.

—Ephesians 1:3

"I am blessed and highly favored!" This was the slogan
that I heard repeatedly growing up in church. Whenever
you would ask someone how they were doing, they would
respond by saying, "I am blessed!" It became so routine
that I just started to repeat the rhetoric even though I really
did not know what it meant.

What does it mean to be blessed? How does one know
when they have been blessed or if they are blessed? What
are the signs of the blessing? We will answer all these very
important questions. In an earlier chapter, we brought

out the fact that the Bible called Joseph a prosperous man when he was actually a slave (see Genesis 39:2). It's probably safe to say that if Joseph was prosperous despite his lack of material possessions, prosperity is not solely defined by material items. The same thing is probably also safe to assume about the blessing. However, the blessing is not just material things but so much more.

As mentioned above, Ephesians 1:3 says that we are blessed with every possible spiritual blessing in Christ in heavenly places. The writer of this epistle (Paul) used a very interesting Greek word for *blessing*: the Greek word *eulogeō*, which means "to praise, celebrate, to invoke a blessing, or cause to prosper."[1] This is an oral pronouncement of favor and prosperity. We get the English word *eulogy* from this word. A eulogy is essentially speaking well over someone who has died. For example, you won't hear a eulogist say, "Roscoe was a horrible person who never took care of his children." Instead, the eulogist will speak a blessing over the person. He will talk about how Roscoe was a great cook or that he loved to hunt or fish, etc.

When you and I became born again, God eulogized us. The old person was co-crucified with Christ and buried with Him in baptism. God pronounced an oral blessing over us in Christ, and this blessing has set spiritual and natural forces in motion that produce the reality of that which has been pronounced. In other words, the blessing produces prosperity in every area of our lives. What is the value of the words God speaks? The Bible says, "Through faith we understand that the worlds were framed by the Word of God so that things which are seen were not made of things which do appear" (Hebrews 11:3). When God said, "Let there be light," everything in the cosmos obeyed His voice. Even the invisible world came into visible manifestation in response to His Word.

This implies that we are and we have what God has spoken over us and about us. We have been given "all spiritual blessings in Christ." How can the universe become everything that God spoke into being while we remain busted and disgusted? I submit to you, my friend, that should never be. We are empowered to prosper; this is an irrevocable spiritual reality.

The Birthright Blessing

In Genesis 27, we see that Jacob and Esau contended for the blessing. This was not a physical transfer of finances but an oral pronouncement of favor and prosperity. Let us take a closer look at what transpired. "Now it came to pass, when Isaac was old and his eyes were so dim that he could not see, that he called Esau his older son and said to him, 'My son.' And he answered him, 'Here I am.' Then he said, 'Behold now, I am old. I do not know the day of my death'" (Genesis 27:1–2).

In Hebrew tradition, the father would release the birthright blessing to the eldest son who was attributed the term *heir* of the father's estate. What should have happened was that Esau went to the field, came back, and received the birthright from his father Isaac. Unfortunately, God had other plans. Instead, Rebekah carried out her elaborate scheme to get Jacob to supplant the birthright from Esau by impersonating his elder brother.

Jacob said to his father, "I am Esau your firstborn; I have done just as you told me; please arise, sit and eat of my game, that your soul may bless me."

But Isaac said to his son, "How is it that you have found it so quickly, my son?"

And he said, "Because the Lord your God brought it to me."

Isaac said to Jacob, "Please come near, that I may feel you, my son, whether you are really my son Esau or not." So Jacob went near to Isaac his father, and he felt him and said, "The voice is Jacob's voice, but the hands are the hands of Esau." And he did not recognize him, because his hands were hairy like his brother Esau's hands; so he blessed him.

—Genesis 27:19–23

Essentially, through an act of manipulation and deceit (hence his name), Jacob defrauded his brother of the birthright blessing. Isaac released a blessing to Jacob. This was not just a financial inheritance or the transfer of land but much more. Notice what the Bible says. "Therefore may God give you of the dew of heaven, of the fatness of the earth, and plenty of grain and wine. Let peoples serve you, and nations bow down to you. Be master over your brethren, and let your mother's sons bow down to you. Cursed be everyone who curses you, and blessed be those who bless you!" (Genesis 27:28–29).

The blessing is spiritual. He spoke over Jacob's future and declared favor over his entire bloodline. This is very powerful. Of course, that birthright blessing includes finances, but the spiritual aspect is the impetus for physical wealth. Jacob successfully stole his older brother's blessing. This seems like a scene from a soap opera, but I can assure you this is the record of Scripture. How did he accomplish this heist? Jacob was able to receive his elder brother's birthright by impersonating his elder brother. The story of Jacob and Esau is actually a spiritual archetype of what took place in our redemption.

Jesus Is the Elder Brother

In order to receive and walk in the supernatural blessing that can only come from God, we receive our birthright the same way that Jacob did—through our Elder Brother. Jesus is our Elder Brother in redemption. The Bible says this: "But put on the Lord Jesus Christ, and make no provision for the flesh, to fulfill its lusts" (Romans 13:14).

The word for *put on* comes from the Greek word *endyō*, which means "to sink into (clothing), put on, clothe one's self."[2] Jacob wore the clothing or the fur of his older brother, and as a result, his father released the blessing to him because he stood in the place of his brother. Friends, God the Father has blessed us because we stand in the place of Christ. That is right! Jesus stood in our place so that we can stand in His place. He took on our sin so that we can take on His righteousness. He became poor so that we, through His poverty, could become rich. (See 2 Corinthians 8:9.)

We must also note that in order for Jacob to wear the skin of an animal that would allow him to impersonate his elder brother, an animal had to die. Blood had to be shed. Interestingly, in order for us to stand before the Father,

Jesus had to shed His blood for us to assume His righteousness. Yes, designer clothing can be very expensive, but what you and I wear before God the Father was literally to die for.

It would be an atrocity for us to reject such a great sacrifice by forfeiting our right to walk in the blessing of God. Imagine being the son of a wealthy billionaire who, instead of choosing to receive the inheritance that his father sacrificed his entire life for, lives in a homeless shelter and barely has the basic necessities. What would you say to such a young man? You would probably tell him to access his inheritance. Well, I am saying the same thing to you: "Access your inheritance!"

Receive Your Inheritance

Ephesians 1:17–18 says the following about the inheritance we have in Christ: "That the God of our Lord Jesus Christ, the Father of glory, may give to you the spirit of wisdom and revelation in the knowledge of Him, the eyes of your understanding being enlightened; that you may know what is the hope of His calling, what are the riches of the glory of His inheritance in the saints."

The truth is that it does not matter how great an inheritance has been given to us in Christ if we do not receive it. Just like the previous example of the son of the billionaire, if he does not acknowledge and appropriate what he has been given, he will live like a pauper even though he has a rich inheritance. In estate law, three primary parties are involved: the testator, the beneficiary, and the executor.

The testator initiates a last will and testament. The testator can draft or write his or her will, or they can have a lawyer do it for them. The beneficiary is the person(s) who receives some advantage or value from the will or trust. The executor is a person or institution appointed by a testator to carry out the terms of their will. In order for a will to be in force, the testator must die. Once the testator dies, the will or testament is in force. The executor then has the legal authority to execute the terms of the will.

God wrote a last will and testament for the church. Jesus was the Testator, the Holy Spirit is the Executor, and we are the beneficiaries. The moment Jesus died on the cross and rose from the dead, the New Testament came into effect. Jesus said, "And I will pray the Father, and he shall give you another Comforter, that he may abide with you for ever" (John 14:16 KJV).

The Bible also says this: "Likewise the Spirit also helps in our weaknesses. For we do not know what we should pray for as we ought, but the Spirit Himself makes intercession for us with groanings which cannot be uttered. Now He who searches the hearts knows what the mind of the Spirit is, because He makes intercession for the saints according to the will of God" (Romans 8:26–27). The word used for *intercession* here is the Greek word *hyperentygchanō*, which means, of course, "to intercede for another," but it also means "to consult or entreat."[3] Intercession is a legal term and gives us insight into the function of the Holy Spirit. He is the one who acts as the Executor of the New Testament.

Paul the apostle wrote this in his epistle to the Corinthian Church: "Now we have received, not the spirit of the world, but the spirit which is of God; that we might know the things that are freely given to us of God" (1 Corinthians 2:12). The Holy Spirit enables us to know (intimately and experientially) the things that are "freely given to us of God." This means without the Holy Spirit, we cannot know what we have received in the inheritance, just like a beneficiary of an estate won't know what they have in their inheritance until they consult with the executor of the will. Unfortunately, children don't actually learn what their parents possessed in terms of assets until probate court.

The death of Jesus released our inheritance, but we must receive that inheritance in order to enjoy the benefits. What are you waiting for? The Holy Spirit is ready and willing to open the eyes of your understanding so that you would *know* what is the hope of His calling and the glorious riches of your inheritance in the saints.

The Mystery of Bar Mitzvah

In Jewish tradition, every teenage boy or girl undergoes what is referred to as a bar mitzvah (for young males) and bat mitzvah (for young girls). This is a sort of rite of passage that every Jewish child is expected to experience all over the world. The word *bar mitzvah* actually means "son of instruction." This ceremony takes place when a boy or girl turns thirteen, and it indicates that they are ready to observe the religious precepts commensurate with their Jewish heritage and identity.

The bar mitzvah has several components, including reciting from the Torah, giving a speech in the synagogue, and receiving blessing and instruction from the rabbi and other elders in the Jewish community. Essentially, it is releasing a blessing over this teenage child in preparation for their life as a Jewish adult. This is very powerful. The community pronounces an oral blessing over the child. They will say, "Goldberg, you will be a successful lawyer. You will graduate at the top of your class, and you will be very wealthy." They then invest financially into the boy or girl to help them start their lives.

Several years later, you will find that Mr. Goldberg is a top lawyer in his field who is also very wealthy. How did that happen? It is the power of the bar mitzvah blessing. Consider this: if the blessing of mere men and women can set such spiritual forces in motion that inevitably ensure success, how much more can the blessing of our heavenly Father do this for us? God has spoken well over us in Christ. He has said that we are blessed and empowered to prosper in every area of our lives.

Just like the oral blessing during the bar mitzvah unlocks financial blessings, so does the blessing that we have received from God. Yes, God is speaking over us and declaring prosperity and success. He is saying, "My son or daughter will fulfill my plan for their lives." This ancient Jewish tradition holds a mystery that unlocks a greater understanding of Ephesians 1. Every person who has accepted Jesus as their personal Savior and Lord has been bar mitzvahed or bat mitzvahed in Christ Jesus. We received a heavenly blessing from the most powerful person in the universe. We must recognize that we are already blessed and receive and walk in that blessing.

Beware of New Age Counterfeit

Just like all things in life, wherever there is an original, you will often find a counterfeit. Years ago, I went on a business trip. During the long layover, I decided to get my shoes shined at the local parlor inside the terminal. As I was getting my shoes shined, I noticed a businessman getting his shoes shined next to me; he was wearing a very nice and expensive watch brand on his wrist. I said, "That is a beautiful watch! That is a dream watch of mine!"

The gentleman looked at me with a polite grin. "Thank you! But you know the only difference between your watch and mine?"

I said, "No, sir!"

He said, "Your watch is actually real!" He went on to tell me that he actually bought the watch in China for seventy-five dollars. This was a watch that retailed for twenty thousand dollars or more. Wow! From a distance, you could not tell the difference, but when he removed the watch and let me hold it, I could feel that it wasn't real.

You have probably gathered that I am a watch aficionado. Yet I was nearly deceived by a very elaborate and detailed counterfeit. Just like that watch, there are many counterfeits to biblical prosperity that, at first glance, appear to be the same.

A New Age mixture has crept into the American Christian Church. This New Age ideology and methodology is focused on manifesting your reality through positive affirmation. People will often refer to the universe. "I had to ask the universe for that job!," or "I manifested the house of my dreams!" Beloved, that is not biblical faith, and it is definitely not biblical prosperity. One is focused on fulfilling your own selfish desires and ambitions; the other is about fulfilling God's desires.

One looks at God as a means to an end; the other sees God as the end and prosperity as the means. In other words, God is not a way to prosperity; He is prosperity. The New Age sees the created, impersonal universe as some omnipotent being, but the truth is that God created the universe. It has no inherent intelligence, divine will, or providence. Praying to the universe is like a farmer praying to a tree he planted. The New Age promotes the worship of self and the pursuit of self-will. Biblical prosperity promotes the worship of God and the pursuit of His will and His agenda. Although they may look similar from a distance, I can assure you, they are not. One is nothing more than a cheap counterfeit.

The Real Power of the Decree

Many Christians have associated legitimate biblical spiritual principles with something worldly or even occultic. In their attempt to fight against counterfeit spirituality, they have unwittingly thrown the baby out with the bath water. Specifically, we must examine the ancient biblical practice of the decree. Job 22:28 says, "And thou shalt decree a thing and it shall be established." Beloved, our words carry supernatural power and authority, and when used biblically, they can unlock biblical prosperity in our lives.

Oxford Learner's Dictionary defines a *decree* as "an official order from a leader or a government that becomes the law."[4] The word *decree* in Job 22:28 comes from the

Hebrew word *gāzar*, which means "to cut, or to divide."[5] The significance of this word is that, essentially, our words are the divider between success and failure, lack and abundance, poverty or prosperity. What divides the rich from the poor is not education. Many of the world's wealthiest people never graduated from college, so traditional education cannot separate successful people from unsuccessful people. The dividing factor, then, is the words they speak. The Bible declares: "Death and life are in the power of the tongue: and they that love it shall eat the fruit thereof" (Proverbs 18:21 KJV).

The difference between death and life is what we speak. This is not some New Age trend or exercise in pop psychology—this is the Word of God. Our words create our world. For example, two people living in the same city can have two totally different realities. One is trying to figure out how they will pick up an extra shift at work to pay their children's school fees, while the other is trying to decide who will do the catering for the housewarming party at their brand-new mansion. Both of these individuals live in the same city while living in different worlds. In the same way, one person can always sing, "Woe is me!" and always looks at the glass as half empty. They constantly speak negative words and make excuses. Another person constantly speaks life and always sees the glass as half full.

Which one do you believe will experience more abundance in their life? You've got that right! I will definitely not be a negative Nelly (no offense intended if your name is Nelly). When we receive and decree the blessings of God, it affects the quality of our lives. What are you speaking?

Your words carry legal authority in the spiritual realm and have the ability to shape your reality.

Change Your Words, Change Your World

Years ago, I was very cynical and negative. At the lowest point in my life financially, I often complained about my circumstances. In my mind, I believed something was happening to me. In other words, I felt like I was the victim of my circumstances. At that time, like so many people today, I did not realize that I was literally shaping my world.

I was driving to church one Sunday and received a notification of insufficient funds on my phone. The notifications kept popping on my screen. The more I saw them, the angrier I became. I was upset at the bank. I was upset at life. While I sat there and pondered my entire existence, the Lord said, "Kynan, why are you angry?" Before I could answer, He followed up with a second question: "Do you trust me?"

To this question I replied: "Yes, Lord!"

He said, "If you trust me, then why are you moved by what you see?" God has a way of asking questions. The truth of the matter was that I didn't trust God. I did not realize that I had placed more confidence in my bank account than I had placed in God, and my thoughts and words reflected that.

The first thing God began to do was to train me how to speak. One of the common misconceptions that people have is that you combat a negative thought with a positive thought. This is not true! You cannot combat a thought with another thought. We combat a negative thought with the Word of God. It is not enough to attempt to *think* differently; we must *speak* differently if we want to see transformation.

Once I had this revelation, I would decree, "I am blessed!" every time I was notified of insufficient funds. I would say, "We have more than enough in the name of Jesus!" I said this every time we couldn't figure out what to do for food. Eventually, something broke. Something shifted. My world began to change when my words began to change.

Earlier, we said that God spoke well over us in the same manner that Isaac spoke well over Jacob. This irrevocable birthright blessing carried massive implications. It was the gift that kept on giving. We said that the word *blessed* as expressed in Ephesians 1 comes from the Greek word *eulogeō*, which is where we get the English word *eulogy*.[6] Typically, a deceased person is given only one eulogy, and once that eulogy has been given, it is over.

On the other hand, God continues to eulogize us in a sense. Once God speaks, His words continue to produce even into eternity. This is why the Bible says in Isaiah 55:11, "So My word that proceeds from My mouth will not return to Me empty, but it will accomplish what I please, and it will prosper where I send it" (BSB).

God's Word concerning our lives cannot and will not return to Him void. He says we are blessed, so guess what; we are blessed! He says that we are favored, so that is exactly what we are, regardless of our circumstances.

God spoke over Abraham, Isaac, and Jacob, and as a result, they became the fathers of many nations. God has spoken over you, and as a result, you are everything He says you are. Now it is your turn to agree with God and say what He has already said.

Reflection Questions

1. What is meant by the term *blessing* in Scripture? What is the significance of the birthright blessing, and why is it so powerful?
2. What are some New Age counterfeits that we should be aware of as Christians?
3. How does the Jewish tradition of the bar mitzvah relate to believers today?
4. What effect do our words have on our spiritual, physical, and financial life?

Prosperity Prayer

Father, in the name of Jesus, I thank You that You have blessed me with all spiritual blessings in heavenly places in Christ Jesus. I have received the birthright blessing through the blood of Jesus; therefore, I am highly favored by God. I declare that I possess true and enduring riches in Christ, and these spiritual riches are the impetus for my ability to receive earthly blessings. All good gifts come from You, Lord; therefore, I thank You that I receive and walk in supernatural abundance. Because You have blessed me abundantly, I choose to speak blessings and not curses out of my mouth. I declare that my life is a conduit for Your Word, and I speak Your Word over every circumstance in my life in the name of Jesus. Amen!

THE LAW OF SEEDTIME AND HARVEST AND COOPERATING WITH THE SPIRIT OF DIVINE INCREASE

While the earth remains, seedtime and harvest, cold and heat, winter and summer, and day and night shall not cease.

—Genesis 8:22

As I drove down this narrow, quiet road, the tires thumped against the asphalt and birds chirped in the air. What a beautiful day and an awesome moment to reflect! While I thought about my wife, children, and issues in the church, I heard the clarion voice of God. "The most important principle you will ever learn in my kingdom is the law of seedtime and harvest!" After that, there was silence.

It was as if God dropped a microphone (so to speak). I wondered what He meant and why it was the most important principle. I had so many questions. I have come to realize that everything that the Lord spoke to me in the car that day was absolutely true. I will explain why in this chapter.

We will look at the supreme importance of the law of seedtime and harvest and how this spiritual law affects every area of your Christian life and even life in general. I will also lay out the framework for how to practically operate in this spiritual law. If you and I are going to walk in biblical prosperity, we must learn to submit to and cooperate with the law of seedtime and harvest.

The Law of the Seed

In Genesis 8:22 above, God told Noah that as long as the earth remained, there would always be "seedtime and harvest." This was a part of the postdiluvian covenant that God made with Noah. Interestingly, eight is the number of new beginnings, and this promise was made at the end of Genesis 8. It was as if God was telling us that from here on out, this is the principle he would operate by in the earth. He was giving humanity another chance, a new beginning. But Genesis 8 is not the first time we see the principle of the seed. In Genesis 1, look at what it says: "Then God said, 'Let the earth bring forth grass, the herb that yields seed, and the fruit tree that yields fruit according to its kind, whose seed is in itself, on the earth'; and it was so" (Genesis 1:11).

101

Many scholars refer to this as the law of first mention. In other words, when something is mentioned for the first time in the Bible, especially in the book of Genesis, a spiritual precedent is being set. We can derive two very important truths from this passage. 1. Every tree has a seed. 2. Every seed is produces after its kind. This essentially means that an apple tree produces apples, which theoretically contain millions of potential apple trees. This also implies that within the seed is nearly infinite potential. In other words, we must understand four key components about the seed:

1. The seed is the harvest concealed.
2. The harvest is the seed revealed.
3. The harvest is the exponential potential of the seed sown.
4. No harvest can come about without a seed.

We said that within every apple seed is the potential for millions of apple trees. But that potential is hidden or concealed in seed form. The only way that a concealed harvest can come into manifestation is by sowing. Once a harvest comes, we can then see the full expression of what was hidden within the seed. So, then, the harvest is the seed revealed.

We also know that a seed doesn't just produce another seed but produces fruit that contains a seed. In other words, the harvest is not just the seed expressing itself in the same form, but it is the exponential expression of that seed. If the seed is the harvest concealed and the harvest is the seed revealed and the harvest is the exponential manifestation of the seed, then we can safely say that there can be no harvest without a seed. I hope you are following me.

The Tree of Knowledge of Good and Evil

If everything in creation works according to the law of the seed, then this gives us greater insight into the magnitude of Adam and Eve's transgression in the garden of Eden. They ate of a tree that bore fruit, which bore seeds, which contain an exponential harvest. This is why Adam and Eve's sin didn't just impact their lives but impacted the lives of everyone who would come thereafter. In other words, when Adam and Eve ate the fruit, there was a harvest of sin that affected the billions of people who would come after them. Sin was introduced into the world through the law of the seed. What started out as the eating of fruit in Genesis 3 grows into full murder by Genesis 4 and a corrupt society thereafter.

The Bible says in Galatians 6:7, "Do not be deceived, God is not mocked; for whatever a man sows, that he will also reap." The first human beings on this planet sowed to their flesh by eating from the Tree of Knowledge of Good and Evil, and as a consequence, death passed on to the entire human race. This teaches us that though we reap *what* we sow, we do not always reap *how* we sow. What would happen if we applied this spiritual law to every area of our lives? Whenever God wants to introduce something into your life, He will first identify its seed because the seed corresponds to the harvest.

The Supernatural Ways of God

If you and I are going to receive from our all-benevolent God, we must first understand His ways. Here is what Isaiah the prophet says in the Bible:

> For as the heavens are higher than the earth,
> So are My ways higher than your ways,
> And My thoughts than your thoughts.
>
> For as the rain comes down, and the snow from
> heaven,
> And do not return there,
> But water the earth,
> And make it bring forth and bud,
> That it may give seed to the sower
> And bread to the eater,
>
> So shall My word be that goes forth from My
> mouth;
> It shall not return to Me void,
> But it shall accomplish what I please,
> And it shall prosper in the thing for which I sent it.
> —Isaiah 55:9–11

Notice the Bible says, "For as the heavens are higher than the earth, so are My ways higher than your ways, and My thoughts than your thoughts." The Scripture clearly says that God has a way of doing things that is higher than the earth. However, what are His ways? He explains it in the next verse: "For as the rain comes down, and the snow from heaven, and do not return there, but water the earth, and make it bring forth and bud, that it may give seed to the sower and bread to the eater."

We can clearly see that God's ways are seedtime and harvest. In fact, seedtime and harvest are God's mechanisms for abundance. Many people all over the world are praying for God to move in their lives supernaturally. Maybe they are asking for a miracle in their finances. Maybe they believe that their business will turn around. Whatever the situation might be, the question remains, "Have you acknowledged His ways?"

The Seed Will Not Return Void

Beloved, I have come to realize that the Word of God will not return void. (See Isaiah 55:11.) This is not only because I have the personal experience to justify my claim but also because the Word of God explicitly says so. In this passage, an analogous reference is made to the seed. God's Word is like the "rain that waters the earth and does not return . . . that it may give seed to the sower."

We can also see that God's Word is the seed as well. Imagine the seed is like a program. This program has been written and engineered with all the instructions to produce a specific outcome. This program has one goal: to produce a harvest. God's Word is unrelenting. His Word is audacious and persistent. Here is a simplified understanding of the process of every seed. Every seed has four stages, although this is not exhaustive.

1. Seed
2. Sprout
3. Flower
4. Fruit

Every seed begins as just that, a seed. Once a seed is planted in the soil, it starts to germinate or sprout. This basically means that the seed develops a root system. Then the seed develops into a small plant where it begins its flowering process. And eventually, the seed develops into a full-grown plant and starts producing fruit. Guess who else is very familiar with this cycle—that's right, the devil. This is why he is constantly after the seed. The enemy seeks to abort or uproot the seed before it can come to the end of its cycle. In essence, if he intercepts the seed, he can intercept or block the harvest.

The Parable of the Sower

In Mark 4:1–14, we see a very powerful parable of the kingdom of God.

> And again He began to teach by the sea. And a great multitude was gathered to Him, so that He got into a boat and sat in it on the sea; and the whole multitude was on the land facing the sea. Then He taught them many things by parables, and said to them in His teaching:
> "Listen! Behold, a sower went out to sow. And it happened, as he sowed, that some seed fell by the wayside; and the birds of the air came and devoured it. Some fell on stony ground, where it did not have much earth; and immediately it sprang up because it had no depth of earth. But when the sun was up it was scorched, and because it had no root it withered away. And some seed fell among thorns; and the thorns grew up and choked it, and it yielded no crop. But other seed fell on good ground and yielded a crop that sprang up, increased

and produced: some thirtyfold, some sixty, and some a hundred."

And He said to them, "He who has ears to hear, let him hear!"

But when He was alone, those around Him with the twelve asked Him about the parable. And He said to them, "To you it has been given to know the mystery of the kingdom of God; but to those who are outside, all things come in parables, so that

'Seeing they may see and not perceive,
And hearing they may hear and not understand;
Lest they should turn,
And their sins be forgiven them.'"

And He said to them, "Do you not understand this parable? How then will you understand all the parables? The sower sows the word."

—Mark 4:1–14

This is one of my favorite parables in the Gospels because of what Jesus Himself said in verse 13, "And He said to them, 'Do you not understand this parable? How then will you understand all the parables?'" In other words, this parable is the key to understanding all the parables of the kingdom. This goes back to what God told me years ago about the law of seedtime and harvest being the most important principle in the kingdom of God.

When I read Mark 4, I finally understood why He said what He said. Everything in the kingdom of God follows the pattern of the seed. Remember, there are four stages to the seed. There are also four types of soil: wayside, stony ground, thorny ground, and good ground. Each soil represents a different condition of the heart and life and varying levels of receptivity to the seed. Ultimately, the soil that can fully receive the seed of the Word can germinate that seed so that it brings forth its predetermined capacity of fruit. Without going into too deep of a Bible study here, we can see from Jesus's explanation that the enemy comes immediately to steal the seed.

The disciples did not initially understand, but Jesus explained this powerful kingdom reality. Basically, He was telling the disciples that this is what the kingdom of God is like. The seed and the system were constant in this parable; the only variable factor was the soil. Whether we like it or not, the law of seedtime and harvest is irrevocable. Either we will submit to this spiritual law, or we will endure consequences for disobeying it.

The Law of the Seed in Redemption

The kingdom of God is not a religious system but is actually a legal system. When a person does not understand the legalities of the kingdom of God, that person may limit or even hinder their ability to enjoy the blessings and benefits of the kingdom of God. He is a righteous Judge (see Luke 18) and presides over the universe. In fact, God is so righteous that He had to use the law of seedtime and harvest to redeem the human race from sin. Since mankind got into trouble due to the law of seedtime and harvest, the only way to undo what man did in the garden was through seedtime and harvest. God foresaw this from the very beginning and even prophesied man's redemption in the garden of Eden.

Look at what the Word of God says: "And I will put enmity between you and the woman, and between your seed and her Seed; He shall bruise your head, and you shall bruise His heel" (Genesis 3:15). Even in God's judgment of the human race, He was displaying both His omniscience and His all-benevolence.

In case you didn't read the end of the story (spoiler alert), Jesus is the seed of the woman sown into the earth (seed stage). He tabernacles among us and lives a sinless life, dies on the cross, and is buried (germination stage). He was resurrected from the dead (flowering stage). Then He ascends to the Father and pours out the Holy Spirit (fruit stage). This is why Jesus said emphatically, "Most assuredly, I say to you, unless a grain of wheat falls into the ground and dies, it remains alone; but if it dies, it produces much grain" (John 12:24). God sowed His Son so that He could legally reap His sons. Glory to God!

If God obeys the law of seedtime and harvest, we cannot ignore it. If the most important problem of the human condition (sin) was addressed with a seed, then we must consider how to address the more trivial matters in our spiritual and physical lives.

The Seed Releases Prosperity

It may be hard to believe that the Bible means exactly what it says, but it does. In the most difficult season in my life, the Lord taught me the power of sowing seed. And by the way, seed is not just money, but it does include finances. Our seed could be our time, talent, and treasures. We have taken very straightforward biblical truths and made them somehow controversial. But Paul the apostle was not being controversial when he stated, "But this I say: He who sows sparingly will also reap sparingly, and he who sows bountifully will also reap bountifully" (2 Corinthians 9:6).

During the time this epistle was written, everyone would have known exactly what he was talking about. In that particular verse of Scripture, he is definitely referring to money. Interestingly, the harvest from that seed is not just money. Look at what this verse says: "And God is able to make all grace abound toward you, that you, always having all sufficiency in all things, may have an abundance for every good work" (2 Corinthians 9:8).

The Bible says that when you and I give generously and faithfully, we will reap a harvest of grace. The word *grace* here (from the Greek word *charis*) means "supernatural favor, blessings, and God's divine ability."[1] It reminds me of Deuteronomy 8:18. God did not promise the ancient Israelites wealth in that verse; He promised them the ability to obtain wealth. Similarly, Paul the apostle is saying that if you sow in radical faith, radical obedience, and radical giving, God will make "all grace" abound toward you.

A Testimony of Miraculous Provision

The Lord dealt with my wife and me about giving. We were tithing, but the Lord said that we should go deeper. I shared earlier that the Lord told me to give my last dime when I was preaching at a church. That one act of obedience changed the entire trajectory of our ministry.

After this, the Lord began to deal with us about sowing radically. So we did just that. We started sowing tens of thousands of dollars into our church and several other ministries, families, and individuals. God was faithful. He took care of all of our needs as a family and as a church community. We never lacked anything.

But that wasn't all. God began to give me strategies on what to do in the ministry. Whatever He told me to do, we did it. My wife would say to me, "Kynan, I believe we are supposed to sow fifteen thousand dollars into this couple!" I'd say, "Okay, honey!" No questions asked. The most amazing thing happened. More income came into the ministry and the church than we had seen in ten years. It was truly supernatural. People called and said, "The Lord told me to give you all this." (It would be a ridiculous amount.) My wife and I had now tapped into another dimension of prosperity. Glory to God!

Give, Expecting Something in Return

My point here is not to brag but to encourage you. God has actually delivered my family from financial slavery, and we could experience that emancipation by surrendering to the Word of God, especially in the area of our finances. Millions of people all over the world are still living in a spiritual, mental, emotional, and financial prison because they do not realize that the price for their freedom has been paid in full, in blood.

Another issue is really bad theology. For example, people sometimes say, "You should give, expecting nothing in return." This is pure lunacy. Nowhere does the Bible encourage us to give, expecting nothing in return. In fact, the Bible says the complete opposite. Jesus said, "Give, and it will be given to you: good measure, pressed down, shaken together, and running over will be put into your bosom. For with the same measure that you use, it will be measured back to you" (Luke 6:38).

Our Lord told us to give with the expectation that it will be given back to us. While it is true that we should not give for the sole purpose of receiving something in return, we are to give, expecting that God will honor His Word. Some of you are probably thinking, *But Jesus said, "Do not let your left hand know what your right hand is doing."* (See Matthew 6:3.) In that particular verse, Jesus is speaking of giving alms. This was specifically referring to money or food given to poor people. Jesus was addressing the issue of hypocrisy, superiority, and human dignity. The Pharisees engaged in the very public spectacle of almsgiving as a show of piety and religious superiority.

Jesus condemned these acts because they were not being done out of a pure heart; they were being done to make themselves look good, and they were humiliating the poor in the process. Whenever we help a person who has less material resources than we have, we must always remember that they are image bearers of God and that we could be in a similar position. Therefore, we are never to make a public spectacle out of helping the poor. Some of your favorite organizations violate this Scripture all the time. However, this has nothing to do with giving and expecting nothing in return. In fact, the Bible says, "He who has pity on the poor lends to the LORD, and He will pay back what he has given" (Proverbs 19:17).

The Danger of False Humility

Years ago, a couple in our church gave a substantial financial gift. They were very clear that we were not to tell anyone how much they had given. We agreed and did not disclose this information.

To our surprise, the couple became offended when we didn't tell people who it was. This is called false humility, and it is very dangerous. We must be very careful not to operate in false humility. Anything in us that desires to be recognized by people for what we do for God alone is deceptive and has the potential to bring us into bondage to offense and rejection.

We must always remember that our reward comes from God. (See Colossians 3:24.) We must also understand that whether we want something in return or not, the irrevocable spiritual law of reciprocity dictates that if the seed is good and the soil is good, there will be an inevitable harvest.

Common Lie: It Does Not Matter What I Give

Another very deceptive ideology floating around in the church is this concept that suggests that it doesn't matter what we give. After all, "God sees my heart!" While we need to understand the significance of our heart posture when giving, we also equally need to look at what God actually requires of us. Giving God one hundred dollars when He has asked you for one thousand dollars is not a matter of "God sees my heart"; it is actually a matter of disobedience. That's right, partial obedience is disobedience. Contrary to popular belief, God actually *does* look at what you give. Mark's Gospel gives the account of the widow who gave all she had.

> Now Jesus sat opposite the treasury and saw how the people put money into the treasury. And many who were rich put in much. Then one poor widow came and threw in two mites, which make a quadrans. So He called His disciples to Himself and said to them, "Assuredly, I say to you that this poor widow has put in more than all those who have given to the treasury; for they all put in out of their abundance, but she out of her poverty put in all that she had, her whole livelihood."
>
> —Mark 12:41–44

Look at what Jesus was doing in this passage. He sat over the treasury and watched to see what people were putting in the offering. What? This should serve as a rude awakening to all those who suggest that it does not matter what you give. Not only did Jesus take inventory of what the people put in the treasury; He actually discussed their giving with His disciples later.

He went further to say that the widow gave more than all the rich people combined because she gave 100 percent of her income. It wasn't about the amount; it was about the proportion. There was a marriage between the heart posture of the widow and her works. Jesus actually praised the woman for giving more than everyone else. She gave out of a posture of sacrifice. This truly moved the heart of Jesus. Let's consider what we have given sacrificially to the Lord lately, what we have given God that really cost us something. Almost every major shift in my life can be traced to a season of sacrificial giving. It does matter what we give.

The Revival of the Fruit Bearers

Every major revival in church history was marked by the emergence of a remnant. Those remnants were radical in their response to the call of God in their generation. We are now on the precipice of yet another revival. Most people would agree that we are in desperate need for a move of the Spirit of God. But what will this move of God look like?

The next Great Awakening will not simply be a move of the Spirit of God in pulpits throughout America but an emergency of anointed men and women of God who are so obedient to the promptings of the Holy Spirit that they are willing to do whatever He says. This will be a revival of fruit bearers, individuals who are fruitful in every area of their lives. These fruit bearers are sacrificial givers. They have an anointing of generosity upon their lives, and God can direct His resources through them at His will. The Father wills that we bear much fruit (see John 15). In order to do this, we must remain connected to God through intimacy and obedience. Our connection determines the fruit that we bear, and the fruit that we bear determines the seed we produce.

You Reap What You Sow

The Bible declares, "Do not be deceived, God is not mocked; for whatever a man sows, that he will also reap"

(Galatians 6:7). As we explore the irrevocable law of the seed, we must understand that whatever we sow, we will reap. This is a blessing but should also be a cause for concern. We need to look at what seeds we are sowing and ask ourselves if we are prepared to reap that particular harvest.

While it is true that we reap what we sow, we do not reap in the same proportion to what we sow. We said before that the harvest is the exponential manifestation of the seed. You will always reap more than what you sow. If I sow dishonor, it will not come back to me in the same measure; it will always be exponentially more. If I sow kindness, it will never come back in the same measure; it will be exponentially more.

Knowing this, it behooves us to take inventory of the seed. Remember, if you plant a seed, you will not get a seed back; you will get a tree that bears fruit that contains multiple seeds.

Reflection Questions

1. What is the law of seedtime and harvest? Why is it the most important principle in the kingdom of God?

2. How does the law of the seed connect us to supernatural abundance?

3. How did God demonstrate the law of the seed in redemption? What was the result?

4. Why does it matter what I give?

Prosperity Prayer

Father, I thank You for Your unfailing love for me. Your Word declares that as long as the earth remains, there will always be seedtime and harvest; therefore, I subject my life and finances to the law of the seed. Father, You are the greatest example of giving in the cosmos. Therefore, as an imitator of You, I am a giver. I give generously and abundantly, according to the measure of faith that You have given me. Everything that I have belongs to You, and I give You permission to direct my resources, time, gifts, and abilities according to Your will and purpose for my life. Your Word declares that where my treasure is, there your heart will be. Therefore, I declare that I yield my heart to You, Lord, and this includes my resources and material possessions. Thank You for Your supernatural abundance in my life in the name of Jesus. Amen!

8

TIRED OF BEING SICK AND TIRED AND RENOUNCING THE VOW OF POVERTY

When Jesus saw him lying there, and knew that he already had been in that condition a long time, He said to him, "Do you want to be made well?"

—John 5:6

Horns were honking, car exhausts popping, and sirens blaring in the distance. It was like an urban symphony of chaos, somehow harmonizing to produce a catchy melody. That night, I was at the very end of myself. Tired, frustrated, and disillusioned, I ran out of sophisticated prayers and complex theological jargon. The only thing I could give was my candor and honesty. I shouted, "Teach me how to prosper!" A part of me was shocked that I would yell toward heaven in such a way. I was a bit nervous as

I pondered whether God would somehow punish me for my honesty. As I stood there quietly, I heard His voice. "I will!" I honestly did not know what to say. God heard my request and answered immediately. At that moment, I realized that class was in session.

That is my dramatic account of the conversation that I had with God that changed my life and was the impetus for this book. I shouted, "Teach me how to prosper!" at God in my most desperate moment. I never knew that those five words would be the catalyst for my exodus out of a life of poverty and bondage, but they were. Like so many people, I was sick and tired of being sick and tired. This is one of the best places a Christian can find themselves. Why? It is a place of humility. It is the place where we finally become teachable and receptive to the Word of God.

Will You Be Made Whole?

In John 5, Jesus met the man at the Pool of Bethesda. The Scriptures do not give us his name, but we know that he had been crippled for a very long time—thirty-eight years. We do not know for sure whether he was born this way, but we do know that his condition was somehow precipitated by sin. (See John 5:14.)

This story has so many dynamics, but I want to focus on the fact that Jesus asked him a profound question: "Will you be made whole?" I have asked thousands of people this same question over the years. And I am asking you this question right now. Will you be made whole? What does this mean? What does wholeness look like? What do you want out of life? I had to ask myself these questions too. We can't continue to make excuses or blame everyone else for our problems. Remember, the man at the Pool of Bethesda wanted to point to others as the source of his problems.

As a chronic victim, I struggled to answer this question. I had to examine myself on a level I had never done before. I had to ask myself what I really wanted out of life. A prophetic question was behind what Jesus asked the man at the Pool of Bethesda. You see, the man at the pool was waiting for healing, but Jesus was offering him so much more. Jesus was offering him wholeness.

Wholeness means that nothing is missing and nothing is broken. To heal the man at the pool would be to restore his ability to walk, but to make him whole would involve addressing the areas in his life that make him susceptible to sickness. If you haven't noticed yet, God loves to ask questions. In Genesis 3, God asked Adam, "Where are you?" In Genesis 4, He asked Cain, "Where is your brother, Abel?" In Exodus 3, God asked Moses, "What is in your hand?"

We know that God is omniscient, so He cannot be asking questions for more information. Since God is all-knowing, we can deduce that he asks questions for the purpose of introspection and self-examination. Jesus desired to restore the man at the Pool of Bethesda to an abundant life; He desires to do the same for you today. Although prosperity is the will of God for your life, we must ultimately make this decision. We must be tired of being broke and desire an abundant life. Are you ready to experience more and greater things? If the answer is yes, then you are ready for a *supernatural megashift* in your life and finances.

The Supernatural Paradigm Shift

When I asked God to teach me how to prosper, I had no idea that He would require me to change the way that I thought about everything. In fact, he required what I call a supernatural paradigm shift. What is a paradigm shift? Before we define a *paradigm shift*, we must first define a *paradigm*. According to the *Oxford English Dictionary*, a *paradigm* is defined as a "typical example or pattern of something; a model."[1] In other words, a paradigm is a pattern of thinking or a model upon which we base our beliefs, perceptions, worldview, and/or behaviors.

God was telling me that you have to have a shift in the pattern that you have come to understand and embrace. In other words, the normal had to become abnormal, and the abnormal had to become normal. Being sick, tired, and broke can no longer be your normal state of existence. "I beseech you therefore, brethren, by the mercies of God, that you present your bodies a living sacrifice, holy, acceptable to God, which is your reasonable service. And do not be conformed to this world, but be transformed by the renewing of your mind, that you may prove what is that good and acceptable and perfect will of God" (Romans 12:1–2).

Paul the apostle appeals to the church at Rome, beseeching them to present their bodies as living sacrifices and to be transformed by the renewing of their minds. I want to emphasize two words here. The first word is *transformed*.

This comes from the Greek word *metamorphoō*, which means "to change into another form, to transform, to transfigure."[2] This is the same word used in Matthew 17:2 when Jesus transfigured before His disciples. He literally changed forms.

The Word of God is commanding us not to be conformed or in the form of the paradigm of the world, but to be transformed into a totally different paradigm. How do we accomplish this? The next part of the verse reveals how: by the renewing of your mind. This is a very powerful Greek word, *anakainōsis*, which means "a renewal, renovation, complete change for the better."[3]

Whenever a contractor renovates a home, he must first demolish the existing structure. Wow! God is asking us to allow our existing thought patterns to be demolished so that He can rebuild them according to His design. This is probably one of the most difficult aspects of a paradigm shift, because we have an affinity for certain thoughts, habits, and patterns, even though they are absolutely toxic and hazardous. We must be willing to let those thoughts and attitudes go so that a true *supernatural* shift can take place in our lives.

Breaking the Cycle of Lack

I did not realize that I had a paradigm that not only accommodated poverty but encouraged it. If you would have told me this years ago, I would have ardently denied it. If prosperity is a spirit, then poverty is also a spirit, and this spirit is manifested in our attitude and demeanor. For example, I always focused on lack, even subconsciously.

Growing up, we went for weeks without power. At times, the water was turned off. I learned to adapt to the insufficiency. When I got married, I often adapted to the lack. I will never forget this particular incident: the death of my grandmother. This marked a shift in my spiritual and financial life. At the time, we were not doing well financially, yet I knew I had to drive up to Georgia to attend her funeral. My late father-in-law had given us a Jeep, but it was not really reliable enough for a six-hour drive. However, I am a man of great faith and power, so I drove that dusty Jeep to Georgia, and it supernaturally made it all the way. Except that's not what happened. It shut down on the side of the road about two hours from my final destination. A tow truck had to come and pick me up.

It took about two hours and fifteen minutes for the tow truck to arrive. The entire ride in the tow truck, all I could do was wonder how much this would cost. Once the car was towed to the mechanic, I had to wait another hour for my father to pick me up. This was quite the adventure. I eventually discovered that it was going to cost about $450 to fix the harmonic balance on my SUV. I didn't even know what a harmonic balance was. Unfortunately, I did not have any money in my bank account. Here I was, nearly seven hours away from home with no money. What was I going to do?

The thought came to me to ask my brother-in-law for the money. Thankfully, he sent the money, and I was able to pay for the truck to be fixed. As simple as this may seem, it was honestly a turning point in my relationship with God and in my finances. I had this sick feeling in my stomach, a feeling of disgust. I finally came to a place where I said,

"Never again!" I made a conscious decision that I would never be at the mercy of someone else financially. I decided to break the cycle of lack in my life.

Sick and Tired of Lack

I do not know if you can relate to my story. I am not sure if you have ever been in that kind of situation. I pray that you can't relate, but if you can, I want you to hear me loud and clear; your life is about to change forever! That situation of financial struggle was the impetus for a transformation. As I continued to allow God to teach me how to prosper, I realized the power of a quality decision.

A quality decision is a decision made that has the power to change the trajectory of our lives. It is a decision made with faith and intention. It is not just an emotional response to difficulty but a decision made when you have counted the cost of change. When you make up your mind what you are willing to pay for something, it is already yours. When we make a quality decision and reinforce that decision by speaking faith-filled words, our circumstances begin to change. I said to myself, "I will never be this broke again." It was as if my life were a radio station and my words were like the tuner.

The more I began to make those declarations, the more my life changed. The key to living in abundance is coming to a place where you are truly sick of lack. Until you develop a hatred for poverty, lack, insufficiency, and defeat, these will always take residence in your life. Whatever you tolerate, you accommodate. Think about the current state of your life. Most things in your life are there

124

because you have permitted them. If you have toxic relationships, you permitted them. If you are constantly experiencing demonic oppression, you permitted it. If you are bound by fear, you permitted it. I do not mean to be insensitive to the people's plight, but I do mean to be biblical. Jesus Himself said, "And I will give you the keys of the kingdom of heaven, and whatever you bind on earth will be bound in heaven, and whatever you loose on earth will be loosed in heaven" (Matthew 16:19).

The word *keys* there comes from the Greek word *kleis*, which means keys that have "the power to open and to shut, or power and authority of various kinds."[4] The word *bind* here (from the Greek word *deō*) means "to bind, tie, fasten or to put under legal obligation."[5] The word *loose* (from the Greek word *lyō*) means "to unbind, release, or discharge."[6] In other words, Jesus gave the church the legal authority to permit or forbid things in the spiritual and natural realms.

Every demonic spirit in our lives needs a permission slip to operate. The moment you and I stop permitting something, it has to leave. I did not realize that poverty was in my life at that time by permission. I gave it permission with my thoughts, words, and actions. Once I realized that the devil was taking up space in my life and that poverty was residing in my mind rent-free, I served him an eviction notice.

Renouncing the Vow of Poverty

Around the thirteenth century, Franciscan monks popularized what is commonly known as the vow of poverty or apostolic poverty. The idea was that poverty and piety were closely related. In other words, the poorer a person was, the more they loved God. As religious as this may seem, the concept is not found in Scripture. In fact, much of this doctrine is rooted in Gnostic dualism (the belief that the physical world is evil and the spiritual world is good).

Of course, we know that the apostle John refutes Gnosticism in his epistles, but many people still somehow embrace the vow of poverty, at least subconsciously. This can easily happen when Scriptures are taken out of context, such as "money is the root of all evil." (The verse actually says "the *love* of money is the root of all evil," but many people conveniently forget to include the first three words. We will deal with the love of money in a later chapter.) The truth is that many people see prosperity as some form of inherent worldliness that should be shunned at all costs. Remember this: You will never attract what you despise or shun as evil. I did not realize that I had subconsciously made a vow of poverty.

I say this because I always experienced this cognitive dissonance when it came to finances. On the one hand, I knew I needed money, but on the other hand, I felt guilty if I desired too much of it. Unfortunately, I am not alone. Many Christians face the same internal dilemma. How can we embrace something when we believe it is ungodly? No good Christian would engage in an activity that they believe violates the Word of God.

The irony about the Catholic vow of poverty (i.e., the belief that one must be poor to please God) is the fact that the Catholic church is one of the wealthiest institutions in the world and has been so for centuries. The Catholic church amassed a tremendous amount of wealth from the poor through the sale of relics, indulgences, and other questionable practices. The Catholic church has a central Vatican bank, a Vatican passport, and a Swiss Guard. They certainly could not afford these things if they were poor. At some point, we have to use common sense.

While millions were being told that poverty is godliness, the church was building multimillion-dollar cathedrals all over the world. This doesn't even make any sense. The idea that the poorer a person is, the more they love God, and the wealthier a person is, the less they love God is absolutely demonic. I have seen evil, poor people and good, rich people; their righteousness had nothing to do with their bank accounts. If we are going to receive the kind of prosperity that God wants to pour out on the church, we must first renounce the vow of poverty that tethers us to lack and insufficiency. Once you renounce the vow of poverty, you can begin to come into agreement with prosperity.

Training for Reigning

My circumstances were a sort of spiritual boot camp or training. I did not realize this at the time, but God was actually teaching me how to prosper in every area of my life. The Lord trained me and showed me that it is His will for me to prosper, be blessed, help the poor, finance missions and churches, provide for my family, give to the kingdom, and more. How can I do those things if I am poor, busted, and disgusted? How can I effect change in my generation if I am constantly struggling and trying to figure out how to take care of myself?

In Genesis 1:26, God said, "Let us make man in our image, after our likeness: and let them (mankind) have dominion . . ." (KJV). God created humankind to reign on the planet earth. We were never meant to be underneath creation, but we were designed to reign over creation. Sin destroyed mankind's ability to function in the original design of God. However, Jesus came to restore that dominion to the people of God. Now we know that ultimate dominion will be restored to the church in the age to come when Jesus ushers in His physical kingdom on earth, but we are called to reign in this life. Look at what the Scripture says: "For if by one man's offence death reigned by one; much more they which receive abundance of grace and of the gift of righteousness shall reign in life by one, Jesus Christ" (Romans 5:17 KJV).

The word *reign* there comes from the Greek word *basileuō*, which means "to exercise kingly power."[7] We are not victims of circumstances, society, or even the economic systems of this world. We are kings and priests to our God through Jesus Christ, and we have authority. We are not supposed to merely survive; we are called to thrive in every area of our lives.

We have been empowered and anointed to reign. What does that look like? It means that we are no longer barely getting by. We are not looking for handouts. The same power that created the universe is at our beck and call. In fact, that power lives in us. From this day forward, you no longer live on "Barely Getting by Street"; today, I declare that you live in victory.

Reflection Questions

1. What was Jesus really asking the man at the pool when He said, "Will you be made whole?"
2. How do we experience significant change in our lives?
3. What does it really mean to be sick and tired of being sick and tired?
4. What is the vow of poverty? How does it affect our ability to prosper?

Prosperity Prayer

Father, in the name of Jesus, Your Word declares that as a man thinks, so is he; therefore, I declare that I possess the mind of Christ. I declare that my mind undergoes a supernatural paradigm shift. You said in Your Word that we are transformed by the renewing of our minds, according to Romans 12:1–2. I renounce the vow of poverty that I may have knowingly or unknowingly subscribed to. I declare that the vow of poverty is an unbiblical doctrine created by men but not created by You. It is Your will that I experience increase and abundance in my life and not lack and poverty. I declare that the false belief of embracing poverty is demonic. I refuse to adhere to any belief system that inherently distorts or denigrates the image of God. As an image bearer of God, I accept my biblical responsibility to reflect your abundance in every area of my life. Amen!

9

SEEKING FIRST THE KINGDOM OF GOD

But seek first the kingdom of God and His righteousness, and all these things shall be added to you.

—Matthew 6:33

My neck tensed as I considered what God was telling me. How could I not be concerned by the continual notifications of insufficient funds that endlessly riddled my phone? What was I supposed to do? When would this stop? I felt like the victim of a violent assault. What would happen tomorrow? Or the day after tomorrow? Yet the still, small voice persisted, "Take no thought for your life." This was one of the most difficult seasons in my life. The difficulty wasn't due to the lack of money but because I was being taught to act in a way that was completely countercultural to how I had been trained my entire life. God was telling and teaching me not to worry. Yet it was almost impossible not to think about my needs when I had so many. This was one of the most powerful lessons that I learned from God.

Dancing to the Beat of a Different Drum

Jesus made a very interesting and provocative statement in Matthew 6. He told His disciples,

> Therefore I say to you, do not worry about your life, what you will eat or what you will drink; nor about your body, what you will put on. Is not life more than food and the body more than clothing?
>
> —Matthew 6:25

Our Lord told us not to even think about our necessities. Wow! I have found that the most requested prayer point in the world is for finances. People write to ministries all over the world, asking for prayer or for help with their children's school fees. Thousands submit requests for God to intervene in their debt or relieve their medical bills. So the number-one prayer request in the world is the very thing God told us not to think about, let alone pray for.

You might think this statement is very insensitive. Yes, it definitely is insensitive if you do not understand the way the kingdom of God operates. The truth is that most people do not know how a kingdom operates because they have never been a part of a kingdom (with the exception of the minority of people who are still a part of a monarchy or dynasty). In America, we are part of what is known

131

as a democratic republic or a representative democracy (which one is an issue of debate). In a democratic society, the people vote for their representatives, and those representatives legislate on matters concerning the people of that society.

However, in a kingdom, the king is responsible for his citizens. He elects these citizens and provides for these citizens. Jesus essentially told His disciples, "In the kingdom of God, I am responsible for taking care of you." It is insulting to a benevolent king to constantly bring our daily necessities before Him. Within the kingdom of God is everything we need.

Ironically, most of our endeavors in life are a consequence of taking thought for our lives. Think about it: Why did you choose your educational path? Why did you engage in that particular career or vocation? Most of the decisions that we make are centered around money (our need for it or lack thereof).

The Mystery of Unlimited Provision

We will discuss the love of money in more detail in a later chapter, but notice that nowhere in Scripture are we encouraged to pray for money. Instead, the essence of all spiritual and physical provision is within the context of seeking first the kingdom of God. Beloved, this is the mystery of unlimited provision. My life was drastically changed when I discovered this truth.

Imagine a king is seeking to expand His kingdom. How would He achieve this? There are only two ways to expand any kingdom: conquest or colonization. Of course, conquest is the militant takeover of territory, and colonization deals with the spread of language, culture, education, and spirituality. If God is a king, which He is, then He expands His kingdom in the same way. We conquer territory that was previously occupied by the devil by preaching the gospel and casting out demons, and we colonize earth with the kingdom of God through teaching and discipleship. What is the kingdom of God? The Bible says, "For the kingdom of God is not eating and drinking, but righteousness and peace and joy in the Holy Spirit" (Romans 14:17). The kingdom of God is the government of God, His influence and power that manifests in every area of life. The kingdom of God consists of righteousness, peace, and joy in the Holy Spirit. Every time we appropriate God's righteousness, peace, and joy, we are expanding the kingdom of God and functioning as His ambassadors. Therefore, if we are His ambassadors, then He is responsible for all our provision. The key to seeing God's unlimited provision is to become preoccupied with His agenda. Simply put, God's will is His bill.

Earlier, we stated that we are ambassadors of Christ. "Now then, we are ambassadors for Christ, as though God were pleading through us: we implore you on Christ's behalf, be reconciled to God" (2 Corinthians 5:20). The meaning of the term *ambassador* is key and is such an important aspect of walking in prosperity. The Britannica defines an *ambassador* as the "highest rank of diplomatic representative sent by one national government to another."[1]

Think about the power of this definition. If we are ambassadors of Christ, then we are, in fact, official diplomats of the kingdom of God. A diplomat never takes care of their own expenses when they are on official government business. They don't pay for their own transportation, accommodations, or food. In fact, a diplomat doesn't even use their own passport—they have a diplomatic passport. If a natural diplomat has benefits and immunity afforded to them by virtue of their position, how much more do we have benefits and immunity as ambassadors of the kingdom of God? This is why Jesus told His disciples to take no thought for their lives. They were being sent out as His delegates, and therefore, He was responsible for all their needs.

When I worked for a college, I often traveled on behalf of the university. They paid for my plane ticket, hotel accommodations, and gave me a per diem allowance for food. I even had a credit card from the university to take care of all my expenses while I was doing official university business. You cannot convince me that the university I worked for had more resources than the kingdom of God. The key to prosperity is not our occupation or education; the key is doing what we have been assigned to do. When we do what we are called to do, we unlock and activate an ambassadorial anointing that causes provision to flow in and through our lives.

The Grace of an All-Benevolent King

We have often heard the expression that God is a good God. Most people would shout amen to that, right? The problem is that our rhetoric is not always congruent with our revelation and our practical application. Millions of people do not believe that God is good. This is evidenced by the fact that many people in the body of Christ are not experiencing personal victory. People should be able to look at your life and see that God is good. They should be able to discern that God is benevolent based on your attitude. If they cannot, if your life is not a testimony of this, then you really don't believe that God is good.

One of the most powerful revelations that I ever received was the truth that God is completely benevolent. Once I came to understand that God is all-good, I came to expect good from Him. I learned to trust in His goodness. As a father of six children, I can tell you for certain that my children will never have to ask me to take care of their needs. I am a good father, and it is my obligation to provide for my children.

My wife and I brought our children into the world, so of course, we will take care of them. Unfortunately, many people have not had the best relationship with their biological fathers. They have experienced the devastation of an absentee father. They have witnessed the challenges that come from a single-parent home. My children will never know what it feels like not to have a father. They will never know what it feels like to have to work themselves to the bone in order to buy school clothes or take care of their basic necessities. I understand the responsibility of being a father.

Am I a better father than God? Absolutely not! God is a gracious and all-benevolent King who has never failed. Once you understand this truth, you will receive His grace—His enabling power and supernatural ability— that is able to cause all favor and earthly blessings to abound toward us. I no longer pray for money; I simply thank my good Father for His provision. I simply pray like this:

Heavenly Father, in the name of Jesus, I thank You for Your miraculous provision in my life. The earth belongs to You and the fullness thereof, the world and they that dwell therein. The silver and the gold belong to You and the cattle on a thousand hills. Therefore, I thank You for supplying all my needs according to Your riches in glory. Right now, I thank You that the angels (who hearken to the voice of Your Word) retrieve every single dollar that is needed to fund this particular project. I thank You for [say the amount] deposited in every account that I own and operate in the name of Jesus.

Anything in my life that I need, I thank God for it because the Bible is clear. "But my God shall supply all your need according to his riches in glory by Christ Jesus" (Philippians 4:19 KJV). It is God's responsibility to supply my needs. He does this according to His riches in the glory. The treasury of heaven underwrites every assignment or endeavor that it sanctions. The problem is that too many people are engaging in activities that are not sanctioned by the King. Your will is your bill.

Ask yourself this question: Am I doing what God has told me to do, or am I doing what I want to do? However, when you know that we serve a God who is good and gracious, you can rest confidently in His will. You can obey God knowing that He has the best intentions for your life. Some people are struggling in their lives and finances because they are the architects of their own lives. They believe it is their responsibility to take care of themselves. These individuals have not surrendered to the grace of God. Whenever we reject the grace of God, we default into striving for our own provision.

Who's Your Daddy Again?

I want to reiterate a point that I made earlier; my children have never had to ask me to meet their needs. If this is true for a natural father, it is even more true of our heavenly Father. The question is: Who is your Daddy? Jesus made a very powerful statement in the Gospels.

> Ask, and it will be given to you; seek, and you will find; knock, and it will be opened to you. For everyone who asks receives, and he who seeks finds, and to him who knocks it will be opened. Or what man is there among you who, if his son asks for bread, will give him a stone? Or if he asks for a fish, will he give him a serpent? If you then, being evil, know how to give good gifts to your children, how much more will your Father who is in heaven give good things to those who ask Him!
>
> —Matthew 7:7–11

Notice that Jesus makes the correlation between a natural father and his child and our heavenly Father and His children. "If evil men know how to give good gifts to their children, how much more shall your Father which is in heaven give good things to them that ask him" (Mark

137

7:11). If you see God as your heavenly Father, then He delights in giving good things to you. I did not realize that at the root of my struggle with poverty was a subconscious belief that God was not all-good. I thought that He was good sometimes, depending on how good I was that week. I did not know that His goodness was not contingent on my goodness.

Blessings began to overtake my life the moment I believed that God was my *good heavenly Father* who delighted in giving me good things. Glory to God! I learned to declare, "Something good is going to happen to me today!" That is simply because I am a child of God. A door has been opened in my life, and a way has been made for me! Just like a child is excited when their father picks them up from school because they know they are going for ice cream, we should look forward to encountering God every single day. Hallelujah! A child doesn't ask a parent, "Dad, will you feed me today? I'll be good, I promise." A good father gives to his children, and the children don't even need to ask. The father knows he needs to feed his children.

Advancing His Kingdom, Receiving His Promises

We said earlier that the key to walking in supernatural abundance is advancing the kingdom of God. When you make His business your business, He makes your business His business. Did you catch what I just said? Every time we position ourselves to advance His kingdom, we position ourselves to receive His promises. Seeking first His kingdom is the posture of prosperity.

Many years ago, I heard a very powerful story. Several intercessors went to Washington, DC, to pray for the nation's capital. While there, someone informed the ambassador to Iraq that they were praying, and he invited them to come and pray in the Iraqi Embassy. When they entered the embassy, Persian rugs, Middle Eastern lamps, and other accoutrements from his country were everywhere. It was as if they had stepped into Iraq. This is because the embassy is an expression of the country it represents. The embassy looks like its homeland.

The same applies to us as believers. We are the embassy of God, and our lives should reflect the kingdom we represent. The more we advance the kingdom of God, the more our lives will begin to look like heaven. Heaven has no lack, and neither should we. I once was an embassy of lack and poverty. I have since been delivered, and I believe God wants you and me to walk in the blessing.

Reflection Questions

1. What does it mean to seek first the kingdom of God? Why is it significant?
2. What does it mean to be an ambassador of Christ? How do we practically operate in this call?
3. How does God show us His all-benevolence?
4. How do we advance the kingdom of God? What are some practical examples?

Prosperity Prayer

Father, in the name of Jesus, I declare that I am an ambassador of Christ, and as an ambassador of Christ, I am a representative of the kingdom of God in every area of my life. Everywhere the soles of my feet tread is a territory of heaven. As an ambassador of the kingdom of God, I have access to unlimited supernatural provision. I seek first the kingdom of God and His righteousness, and all the things that I need and desire are added to me. I declare that I am preoccupied with the agenda of the kingdom. I declare that You are an all-benevolent and loving God, and You continue to manifest Your love and grace in every area of my life in the name of Jesus. I declare that I walk in a fresh anointing as an ambassador of Christ in Jesus's name. Amen!

10

WHY AM I BROKE?
ASKING THE *HARD* QUESTIONS

For if we would judge ourselves, we should not be judged.

—1 Corinthians 11:31 KJV

He walked by my kiosks several times a day, staring at me with an interesting grin. On this particular day, he nodded his head in contempt. As he pushed the trash can down the terminal, I wondered who this man was. "You aren't doing what you are supposed to do!" he exclaimed. "You need to pray!" At this point, he seemed condescending.

Who does this old janitor think he is? Despite my internal protest, I could not help but feel the weight of his words. I wondered why he spoke to me and what

141

God was trying to say. His words provoked anger and self-examination.

God sent an angel to challenge me to be dissatisfied with where I was in life. At the time, I was working at the airport making ten dollars an hour. I didn't have a car or my own place, but I was working every day. Along comes a man who I believed was an angel sent by God to move me out of a season of lack. This was many years ago, but this encounter still resonates with me to this day.

Why am I broke? I had asked myself that very difficult question many years ago. It is what I call an accountability question. Whenever God wants to change our lives, He will often ask an accountability question. These questions cause us to examine ourselves. Self-examination is the prerequisite to elevation. God will never allow you to go higher in life until you are willing to go under the microscope. In this chapter, we will challenge several areas that may be keeping you from experiencing all that God has for you. If you are willing to be honest and teachable, you will experience a shift into a place of abundance.

The Blame Game

The first thing that we need to address before we go further is what I call the blame game. This is the tendency for people who are not experiencing the life they want to shift blame to someone or something else. I am very familiar with the blame game because I was an expert at playing it. In fact, I was an international gold medalist in the game of blaming others.

Maybe you have said, "I am struggling with finances because the economy is bad." Or maybe you have played the race card: "I am struggling because I am a particular ethnicity, and this ethnicity is unfairly treated." You might have played the age card: "It is because I am a senior citizen," or "I am too young." This one is my favorite: "I am on a fixed income." Any of these and more can be excuses for why you are not where you need to be in life.

The irony of the blame game is that there are no winners, only losers. In this season, you must resolve that you will not play the blame game. Every time we make excuses for why our lives are not where they should be, we inadvertently abdicate our spiritual authority. Read this carefully. Any thought that makes you a victim originates from hell. You must determine in your heart and mind that God's Word is your final authority. The government is not your final authority, the economy is not your final authority, and your upbringing or experience is not your final authority.

The Day I Stopped Being Black

Years ago, I was car shopping in Tampa at a luxury car dealership. Honestly, I used the word *shopping* very loosely; I was really just looking. The salesperson refused to acknowledge me or interact with me. In my mind, this was a classic case of racial discrimination. She was clearly treating me this way because I was Black. That's right! She was a racist, and I was being oppressed. In my anger and frustration, I asked God, "When will you take the reproach of Black people away?" I could hear the "Eyes on Prize" theme music in the back of my mind. I really thought I was fighting for justice.

To my surprise, the Lord answered my question. "I already took your reproach away by the sacrifice of My Son, Jesus. Second, no one has power over you except what you give them. And finally, you are not Black. You are a speaking spirit made in my image, and you have no limitations." Woah! This was a lot to process. The part that I had a particularly hard time with was the last statement that He made. "I am not Black!" I thought, *Then what am I?* What was I going to tell my wife? "Honey, guess what? I am not Black!"

The truth was, my entire identity and personality had been built around the color of my skin. Somehow, I knew exactly what God was saying to me. He was telling me that my spiritual identity was greater than my physical identity. In Christ, we have become the one new man. (See Ephesians 2:15.) I realized at that moment that I was no longer a slave to the amount of melanin in my skin. I was no longer a victim.

Please do not misunderstand me. I am not suggesting that I do not appreciate my culture or the color of my skin, but those things do not determine who I am. My earth suit is not my identity; neither is your earth suit your identity. I am not Black; you are not white or whatever hue that you identify with.

This has everything to do with walking in prosperity. Once you recognize that in Christ you are not a victim anymore, you can begin to receive everything that God has for you, regardless of the limitations that society attempts to place on you. You are not limited by your ethnicity, skin color, nationality, gender, age, or any other factor that the devil tries to use to hinder you from an abundant life. Of course, an eight-year-old girl can't be the men's weightlifting champion, but you get the picture.

God's Will concerning Your Finances

I have said several times that God's will is His bill. Simply put, God finances His agenda. The more we align with God's agenda, the more we see His provision in our lives and finances. We must know God's will concerning our finances. Faith can only operate where the will of God is known. If a person is ignorant of the will of God in a particular area of their lives, they will not be able to confidently exercise biblical faith in that area. For example, if you do not know that God's unconditional will is for you to walk in divine health, you will have a difficult time resisting sickness and believing in healing.

The same is true of your finances. If you do not know beyond the shadow of doubt that it is the unconditional will of God for you to walk in prosperity, you will not resist the spirit of poverty and believe in God for abundance in your life. You must make up your mind that God wants you blessed! Say that with me, "God wants me blessed!" Do you believe that? You know that this is His will because the Word of God is the will of God. Here is what the Bible says.

> Praise the Lord!
> Blessed is the man who fears the Lord,
> Who delights greatly in His commandments.

His descendants will be mighty on earth;
The generation of the upright will be blessed.
Wealth and riches will be in his house,
And his righteousness endures forever.

—Psalm 112:1–3

The Bible explicitly says that the man who fears the Lord will possess wealth and riches. Woah! That can't be right, can it? Why yes, yes, it *is* right! That is exactly what the Bible says. In fact, this is such an important passage of Scripture that Paul the apostle quotes from it directly in 2 Corinthians.

And God is able to make all grace abound toward you, that you, always having all sufficiency in all things, may have an abundance for every good work. As it is written:

"He has dispersed abroad,
He has given to the poor;
His righteousness endures forever."

Now may He who supplies seed to the sower, and bread for food, supply and multiply the seed you have sown and increase the fruits of your righteousness, while you are enriched in everything for all liberality, which causes thanksgiving through us to God.

—2 Corinthians 9:8–11

Paul quotes directly from Psalm 112:9. "He has dispersed abroad, He has given to the poor; His righteousness endures forever; His horn will be exalted with honor."

146

If this promise were just relegated to the Old Testament, then why would Paul the apostle use this very Scripture to substantiate his claim that God will bless those who sow? This is an irrevocable promise from the Word of God. It is God's will for you to prosper in your finances. You must get this deep down in your spirit. The Bible says that faith comes by hearing and hearing by the Word of God (see Romans 10:17). Once you have heard what the Word of God has to say on the subject of finances, faith can come.

God's Spiritual Laws concerning Giving

As I have reiterated many times throughout this book, the law of seedtime and harvest is God's mechanism for increase. This law is irrefutable and irrevocable. Honestly, it surprises me how many Christians blatantly violate this spiritual law and wonder why they are still broke. If a person never drank water or never ate any food, of course, their energy would be low. A better example is a farmer who never plants any seed and wonders why he doesn't have a harvest at the end of the year. The harvest is the inevitable consequence of the seed.

The Bible is clear: "Do not be deceived, God is not mocked; for whatever a man sows, that he will also reap" (Galatians 6:7). You must grasp this vital spiritual principle: Your standard of giving determines your standard of living. In the kingdom of God, how you give determines how you live.

A very well-to-do man once walked up to me and handed me a twenty-dollar bill. "That's for you, sir!" He was so happy with himself. You could see the joy on his face. He thought he really made an impact on my life. Please don't misunderstand me; I am grateful for everything I receive from God, but I am trying to highlight a serious error in the body of Christ. People believe that it doesn't matter if or what they give. This serious doctrine of demons has crept into many denominations and Christians circles. So many Christians tip God and think they are doing Him a huge favor. This mentality is a sure path to the pit of poverty. Jesus said, "For where your treasure is, there your heart will be also" (Matthew 6:21).

We need to consider what our treasure is, what we value or esteem highly. We cannot say that God is first in our lives if we don't reflect this truth in our giving.

The Irrevocable Law of Generosity

The Bible says, "My people are destroyed for lack of knowledge. Because you have rejected knowledge, I also will reject you from being priest for Me; Because you have forgotten the law of your God, I also will forget your children" (Hosea 4:6). People often quote this verse. But contrary to popular belief, ignorance is not bliss. What we do not know can have a damaging effect on us.

The Bible says that the lack of knowledge brings destruction. Why? The Scripture tells us: "Seeing thou hast forgotten the law of thy God." Notice that the ignorance here is not just a lack of knowledge or information, but it is the forgetting and neglecting of God's law. Many people are suffering unnecessarily in their finances because they have refused to adhere to God's laws.

When we talk about a law, we are talking about the system of rules that a particular country or community recognizes as regulating the actions of its members and which it may enforce by the imposition of penalties. Contrary to many people's theology, the spiritual laws of God were not abolished as a result of the cross. Jesus fulfilled the Mosaic law and paid the penalty for our sins, but He did not abolish our spiritual responsibility to obey spiritual laws. In fact, the Bible says, "For the law of the Spirit of life in Christ Jesus has made me free from the law of sin and death" (Romans 8:2). There is a law of the Spirit of life. There is a law of faith (see Romans 3:27).

Spiritual laws must be obeyed in order for us to enjoy an abundant spiritual life. The law of generosity is no exception. Here is the law of generosity: "But this I say: He who sows sparingly will also reap sparingly, and he who sows bountifully will also reap bountifully" (2 Corinthians 9:6).

1. I reap in proportion to what I sow.
2. There is no harvest without a seed.
3. The more generous I am, the more room I make to receive from God.
4. God is obligated to give seed to the sower.

The more generous I am, the more heaven involves itself in my financial affairs. When you embrace a life of generosity, you position yourself in a state of constant reaping. Whatever you give increases, and whatever you withhold decreases. This is another very important aspect of the law of generosity: God cannot multiply what you hold or hoard, only what you sow and give.

Whose Hands Is It In?

One of my favorite stories in the Gospels is the story of the two fish and five loaves of bread.

> When it was evening, His disciples came to Him, saying, "This is a deserted place, and the hour is already late. Send the multitudes away, that they may go into the villages and buy themselves food."
>
> But Jesus said to them, "They do not need to go away. You give them something to eat."
>
> And they said to Him, "We have here only five loaves and two fish."
>
> He said, "Bring them here to Me." Then He commanded the multitudes to sit down on the grass. And He took the five loaves and the two fish, and looking up to heaven, He blessed and broke and gave the loaves to the disciples; and the disciples gave to the multitudes. So they all ate and were filled, and they took up twelve baskets full of the fragments that remained. Now those who had eaten were about five thousand men, besides women and children.
>
> —Matthew 14:15–21

This story includes so many elements, but I want to focus on the aspect of possession. Notice that the two fish and five loaves of bread in the hands of the young lad were simply enough to satisfy his lunch. The two fish and five loaves of bread in the hands of the disciples were only enough to perplex the disciples. Yet once the two fish and five loaves of bread came into the hands of the Master, they were enough to feed nearly fifteen thousand people. This entire scenario was dependent upon whose hands the resources were in.

A basketball in my hands might win a few recreational games, but a basketball in the hands of Michael Jordan can win six NBA championships. A golf ball in my hands can barely compete against an experienced golfer, but a golf ball in the hands of Tiger Woods can win five Masters Tournaments (the second highest since 1934).[1] It all depends on whose hands it's in.

The key to this miracle of multiplication is in the phrase "bring them to me." What have you kept in your hands and refused to bring to Him? Whatever it is, it is holding up your prosperity. As long as you hold it in your hands, you are actually suffocating your future harvest. As we position ourselves to experience the abundant life, we must be willing to relinquish possession of the things we hold dear. God wants to take what is in your hands and use it to feed the multitudes. Will you let Him?

The Law of Stewardship

Another very important spiritual law (along with the law of generosity) that you and I must respect and obey is the law of stewardship. Since the garden of Eden, God implemented this spiritual law in the earth. He told Adam to till the ground, to dress it and to keep it. Based on Adam's faithfulness with the first assignment of naming the animals, He saw fit to entrust him with a wife. The measure of prosperity that we are able to receive is based upon our level of stewardship. God doesn't just give you what you want; He gives you what you have the capacity to steward. This is what the Bible says:

For the kingdom of heaven is like a man traveling to a far country, who called his own servants and delivered his goods to them. And to one he gave five talents, to another two, and to another one, to each according to his own ability; and immediately he went on a journey. Then he who had received the five talents went and traded with them, and made another five talents. And likewise he who had received two gained two more also. But he who had received one went and dug in the ground, and hid his lord's money. After a long time the lord of those servants came and settled accounts with them.

So he who had received five talents came and brought five other talents, saying, "Lord, you delivered to me five talents; look, I have gained five more talents besides them." His lord said to him, "Well done, good and faithful servant; you were faithful over a few things, I will make you ruler over many things. Enter into the joy of your lord." He also who had received two talents came and said, "Lord, you delivered to me two talents; look, I have gained two more talents besides them." His lord said to him, "Well done, good and faithful servant; you have been faithful over a few things, I will make you ruler over many things. Enter into the joy of your lord."

Then he who had received the one talent came and said, "Lord, I knew you to be a hard man, reaping where you have not sown, and gathering where you have not scattered seed. And I was afraid, and went and hid your talent in the ground. Look, there you have what is yours."

But his lord answered and said to him, "You wicked and lazy servant, you knew that I reap where I have not sown, and gather where I have not scattered seed. So you ought to have deposited my money with the bankers, and at my coming I would have received back my own with interest. So take the talent from him, and give it to him who has ten talents.

"For to everyone who has, more will be given, and he will have abundance; but from him who does not have, even what he has will be taken away. And cast the unprofitable servant into the outer darkness. There will be weeping and gnashing of teeth."

—Matthew 25:14–30

The kingdom of God is a governmental system established upon righteousness, peace, and joy in the Holy Ghost. The kingdom of God is also established on the law of stewardship. In the Gospel of Matthew, Jesus told us, "For the Kingdom of Heaven is as . . ." This is what we call a parable. The *Oxford Dictionary of Words* defines a *parable* as a "simple story used to illustrate a moral or spiritual lesson as told by Jesus in the Gospels."[2] The purpose of this parable was to illustrate the kingdom.

The Lord traveled and gave His servants talents "according to their abilities." One received five talents, one received two, and the last received one. We know the story. Each man stewarded his talents and was rewarded with more, except the servant who only received one talent. He buried his talent, and the Lord called him wicked. One of the points that many people ignore in this parable is that the servant who received one talent buried it out of fear and a negative perception of his Master.

The Mystery of the Talents

Why is the parable of the talents such a significant parable in the Gospels? This parable holds the secret to supernatural abundance. In the parable, the Lord audited His servants to see what they did with what He gave them. In other words, what they received next was contingent upon what they did now. Your next is always determined by your now. What have you done with what God already gave you? How are you investing your time, talents, and treasures? How you manage what is in your hands now will determine how much God can entrust you with.

Poverty is not about not having; it is about not knowing the value of what you already have. In the same way, prosperity is not about having an abundance of material possessions; it is really about recognizing the value of what you possess. If you want a house, you must properly steward the apartment that you already have. If you want a new car, you must correctly steward the used car that you already own.

You can indicate your readiness for more by properly stewarding what you already have. When my wife and I started the church, we actually did everything. My wife was the children's church leader, the worship leader, and the usher. I was the preacher and the sound technician.

Our first sound system was a computer speaker under a chair, and we used it every Sunday. Then God gave us a three-hundred-dollar PA system. We had to purchase it from a sound-equipment store on credit. That precious business owner allowed us to pay over time until it was paid in full. We paid the balance on time. God was testing our faithfulness. Every Sunday, I went to the hotel early and set up the sound system. I kneeled down and placed electrical tape over the wires. After I set up the sound system, I interceded over the room and prepared to preach, and I preached my heart out! God was testing our faithfulness. I had no idea that I would eventually have hundreds of thousands of dollars' worth of equipment and a full staff. God knew what He was going to give us, but we had to demonstrate faithfulness in the little things.

Are you faithful with five dollars? Are you faithful with fifty dollars? Are you faithful with fifty thousand dollars? Do you understand? What has God entrusted to your care? Have you demonstrated faithfulness in those things? Your stewardship will determine your readiness to receive and how much you are able to receive from Him. Have you been a good steward?

What Is Your Attitude about Finances?

Earlier, we spoke about the difference between the scarcity mindset and the abundance mindset. Your stewardship as a believer is based upon your mindset. Our ability to receive and walk in the abundance of God is a mindset. I challenge you today to think of what you have as more than enough, just like the two fish and five loaves of bread were more than enough to feed the multitudes once they were in the right hands.

My late pastor started a real-estate business with $250 and turned it into millions of dollars. He knew the value of managing resources and the right mentality. Whatever you appreciate appreciates (increases in value), and whatever you despise depreciates (loses value). God wants to take what you have right now and multiply it. The key is possessing the right mental attitude.

We need an attitude of gratitude, gratefulness for whatever is in our bank account right now. What we have is a result of the grace of God. Whenever we have a scarcity mindset concerning finances, we never have enough. That negative attitude causes a person to constantly focus on what they do not have versus focusing on what they do have. This is why generosity is such a powerful force in the life of a believer. Every time we yield to a spirit of generosity, we are telling God that we can handle more of what He has given us. Contrariwise, every time we hoard what is in our bank accounts, we are telling God that we are incapable of receiving more.

Your attitude is a consequence of your mentality, and your mentality is a consequence of the words you constantly speak. I used to say, "That is too expensive!" "That costs a lot of money!" This was the manifestation of a scarcity mindset. When it comes to finances, the issue is never whether something costs too much; the issue is always "Is this God's will?" "Is this an exercise in good stewardship?" If your child's education were expensive, but it was exactly what they needed, you would not hesitate to invest in their schooling. You must never make any decision solely on the basis of money. Always make decisions based upon the wisdom of God.

Reflection Questions

1. Why is it important to ask ourselves hard questions? What are the benefits of asking these questions?
2. What is biblical stewardship? How do I know that I am being a good steward of the resources God has given me?
3. What are the biblical laws concerning giving? Why are they important?
4. What is the will of God concerning my finances?

Prosperity Prayer

Father, in the name of Jesus, I recognize that You are a generous God. In fact, You are the most generous person in the universe. I declare that my life is completely submitted to the irresistible law of generosity. Every area of my life is saturated in Your supernatural love. I declare that I am empowered to be a good steward of Your resources, Lord. I declare that my life is flourishing and prosperous, according to the Word of God. I declare that Your will is accomplished in my finances and that I am anointed to be a destiny helper to the people that You send to me. I declare that I am the head and not the tail and that I am blessed to be a blessing in the name of Jesus. Amen!

11

THE LOVE OF MONEY . . .

For the love of money is the root of all evil: which while some coveted after, they have erred from the faith, and pierced themselves through with many sorrows.

—1 Timothy 6:10 KJV

As I passed by each luxury car, I enumerated the nefarious and diabolical occupations of each of the car owners. "Drug dealer! Gang banger! Extortioner!" The nicer the vehicle, the more criminal attributes the owner probably possessed. At least, that's what I told myself. Otherwise, they would not be able to afford such nice cars. After all, there's no way anyone could afford these kinds of luxury goods in this economy. The more I speculated, the more frustrated I became. I racked my brain, thinking about all the possibilities. Yet there was an emptiness in my heart, a numbness inside. I had accused these people that I didn't even know of loving money, when in reality, I was the one who was in love with money.

That was a real scene from the story of my life. Years ago, my wife and I were walking through a movie theater parking lot. At that time, I did not have a car. My wife would pick me up, and we would drive around Tampa. On this particular night, we decided to go see a movie. I have always loved cars, and a fleet of luxury cars was parked outside the theater in South Tampa (a very high-end neighborhood).

How could people afford these kinds of cars? I became very angry! My mind descended to a dark place of judgment and criticism. But really, I loved money more than they did. At that moment, I realized that the Bible doesn't just say that the love of money is relegated to the rich, but the poor can love money as well. What does it mean to love money? Let's explore the concepts of what it means to love money and why the Bible says that the love of money is the root of *all* evil in greater detail in this chapter.

You Cannot Serve God and Mammon

One of the most powerful Scriptures on the subject of money is found in Matthew's Gospel. "No one can serve two masters; for either he will hate the one and love the other, or else he will be loyal to the one and despise the other. You cannot serve God and mammon" (Matthew 6:24).

Mammon was more than money; it was actually a god that people worshiped. Mammon was the god of daily provision. Jesus said it is impossible to worship God and mammon simultaneously.

This truth became very vivid to me several years ago. At the time, we were just starting out in ministry. With a very small amount of savings, I walked away from a corporate job. We honestly spent that money very quickly, and we were down to nothing. We struggled to go back and forth to church, provide for the kids, or even purchase food, and we were using food stamps to buy groceries. We truly had to believe God for every penny.

One day, I was watching a television broadcast. An interview with someone named Joan Hunter came on, and she was talking about her journey out of poverty and about God's miraculous provision. My spirit was so stirred as she spoke, I began to pray. We started telling the few members in our church about God's miraculous provision, even before we had a full understanding of the revelation behind it.

One night, as I was sitting in my living room praying, the Lord began to speak to me. He made the most shocking statement I had ever heard up to that point: "You love mammon!" What? He said it again. "You love mammon!" I didn't understand how this could be. How was it possible for someone who didn't have any money to love mammon?

First, we must define *love*. The thing you love is what you spend most of your time and effort on. It is what you think about the most. I realized that I always thought about money. I always focused on my needs being met. When I looked at it from that perspective, I realized that I did indeed worship mammon. Oh my!

At that moment, I prayed a very simple prayer, "God, please forgive me for worshiping mammon! I repent!" Forty minutes later, we received a knock on the door. It was one of our church members. He said that exactly forty minutes earlier (they lived approximately forty minutes away), God spoke to them and told them to get in their car and bring us one thousand dollars. Glory to God! In the same moment I renounced my love for mammon, my money was released.

Mind on My Money and Money on My Mind

A popular song in the nineties said, "I have my mind on my money and my money on my mind" (my paraphrase). As cliché as this phrase was, it alluded to the idolatry of money. One of the first commandments God gave to His people was to have no other gods before Him. Whatever we put in the place of God in terms of our affections and attention is, in fact, an idol. We cannot serve God and money.

The Bible says that the *love of* money—not money itself—is the root of all evil. Whatever we worship instead of God becomes a source of evil in our lives and in society as a whole. People lie, cheat, steal, and kill over money. Children are trafficked over money. Marriages are destroyed over money.

Yet the Bible says that money answers all things. (See Ecclesiastes 10:19.) Money can solve the problem of education. Money can put a roof over a person's head. Money has the power to alleviate the issue of hunger. But when it becomes more than what it was intended to be, we are in serious trouble. Anything we make an idol of will elude us, including money. In fact, it is countercultural to the kingdom of God to chase money. We were not meant to run after blessings or money. The blessings are meant to pursue and overtake us as we run after God.

We pervert God's purpose when we make money our pursuit. Yet millions of people, including Christians, make money their main focus. They beg God for money, languish when they don't have it, and judge others who they believe have more of it than they do. I know this cycle well because I was caught in it for years. My mind was on my money, and my money was on my mind, even though I didn't seem to have much of it. I had unwittingly become its slave—mammon was my master even though I was declaring emphatically that Jesus was Lord. The irony was that this was happening subconsciously.

Many of us have been classically conditioned to pursue money and success at all costs. Even subconsciously, our choices in education, job positions, and even spouses are often motivated by finances. However, God wants to be the motivating factor for every decision in our lives. When making decisions, ask yourself these questions. How will this job bring me closer to God's purpose for my life? How does this spouse align with God's will? What direction does God want my life to take? As simple as these questions may seem, this is a supernatural secret to releasing unlimited prosperity and abundance in our lives. I declare that your mind is on God and God is on your mind, in the name of Jesus. Hallelujah!

Our Passionate Pursuit

When the Lord showed me the supernatural vision of the treasury of heaven, I realized that God has an endless supply of every resource that we need. To corroborate this truth, the Bible explicitly states: "As His divine power has given to us all things that pertain to life and godliness, through the knowledge of Him who called us by glory and virtue" (2 Peter 1:3).

He has given us *all things* that pertain to life and godliness. The idea that God wants to save our souls and doesn't concern Himself with our daily needs is not only erroneous but is actually a demonic doctrine. At its root is a perversion of the understanding of the all-benevolence of God. We spoke earlier about the truth that God is a good Father who gives good gifts to His children. This clearly does not align with the belief that God wants you to suffer in life in order to bring His name glory. He is the lover of our souls who passionately pursues us and desires that we passionately pursue Him in return.

What is your pursuit? What are you chasing? Things are inanimate; therefore, if we chase things, we are actually not moving at all. Many people are experiencing unusual and unnecessary delays in their lives because they are not pursuing the things of God.

For years, I thought that if I could just make six figures, I would have arrived. Surprisingly, I achieved my goal of six figures, and I didn't feel any different. Then I thought, *If I can just reach one million dollars, then life will really be great.* Guess what? I reached one million dollars, and it didn't feel any different. That's because the goal was never a particular amount of money (although there is nothing wrong with setting specific financial goals); the goal was to fulfill the assignment that God had given me. The problem was, like so many people, I did not know the goal. The will of God should always be our ultimate pursuit. Money is a result of that pursuit. As counterintuitive as this may seem, it is absolutely biblical. Look at what the Word of God says:

> This Book of the Law shall not depart from your mouth, but you shall meditate in it day and night, that you may observe to do according to all that is written in it. For then you will make your way prosperous, and then you will have good success.
>
> —Joshua 1:8

This verse says that we should meditate on God's Word day and night, and then we will make our way prosperous and have good success. The problem in American society is that people want to divorce their pursuit of "good success" from "this book of the law shall not depart out of your mouth."

The word *meditate* comes from the Hebrew word *haga*, which means to "ponder, speak over, or mutter under your breath."[1] It means to speak something over and over again. Meditating on the Word of God is His secret to releasing prosperity and success in your life. Remember, prosperity is not the pursuit; it is the result.

Money Is Not Evil or Good

A very important point to highlight in this conversation is the fact that money is neither evil nor good. Money is amoral. Money takes on the nature of the person wielding it. This is why Jesus said, "Therefore if you have not been faithful in the unrighteous mammon, who will commit to your trust the true riches?" (Luke 16:11).

The word *unrighteous* there comes from the Greek word *adikos*, which means "one who violates or has violated justice, unjust, unrighteous, sinful, of one who deals fraudulently with others, deceitful."[2] This comes from the Greek root word *dikē*, which means "custom, usage, or justice."[3] It is a legal term for how a judicial hearing is carried out. When Jesus referred to the unrighteous mammon, He was actually referring to money or riches that are used unjustly or for fraudulent purposes.

When you go to the store and the clerk gives you money out of the cash register, that change did not come from heaven. That money was not deposited by angels. Prostitutes patronized the same store as you. The Bible says that we must be "faithful" with unjust riches. The purpose that money is used for either sanctifies it or corrupts it. The Bible says, "A good man leaves an inheritance to his children's children, but the wealth of the sinner is stored up for the righteous" (Proverbs 13:22).

A trafficker will build perverse hostels with money. A Christian missionary will build an orphanage with the same money that touched the hands of the trafficker. Whose hands is money in? This is why every time we shun prosperity, we are saying that we would rather the money be in the hands of wicked people.

A great transfer of wealth is coming to the body of Christ, but wealth will not be transferred from selfish sinners into the hands of selfish Christians. God is looking for a *generous generation* whom He can trust to direct His resources according to His will.

Money Is Meant to Be Managed

The Lord spoke to me. "Kynan, money is an instrument that empowers decisions." I immediately knew what God was saying. When I was in art school, we were given a medium kit that consisted of canvas paper, charcoal, watercolors, oil-based paint, pencils, etc., to complete our projects. If I had to do a project that required charcoal on canvas, I would pull those resources from my kit to create the desired artwork.

Money is the same way; it is a tool. We use it to fund, finance, and underwrite various things in our lives and in the lives of others. We were responsible as students for managing our medium kit, and in the same way, we, as Christians, are responsible for managing money. Whatever you fail to manage will manage you. Whatever you neglect to take dominion over will take dominion over you. You cannot manage something when you are afraid of it or if you believe it is inherently evil. Money was never meant to be loved; it was always meant to be managed. When the righteous steward money, it can advance the kingdom of God. The Bible is very clear about this.

> And you shall remember the Lord your God, for it is He who gives you power to get wealth, that He may establish His covenant which He swore to your fathers, as it is this day.
>
> —Deuteronomy 8:18

You read that right. God gives us the power to get wealth so that we can establish His covenant in the earth. We can deduct from that passage that the purpose and covenant of God cannot be established without wealth. Like any tool, money must be wielded carefully so as not to harm the one wielding it or the people it affects.

Have you managed money properly? Have you been a good steward of God's resources? Can God trust you with more? Do you know how to handle the unrighteous mammon?

We said earlier that the word *power* there actually means the "ability of angels."[4] God has endowed us with the supernatural grace and ability to obtain and manage wealth.

This is why we do not need to be afraid of wealth, but we must respect it. Whatever you respect, you attract. Whatever you disrespect, you repel. The same principles that apply to spiritual matters apply to finances. The reason many people don't have money is because they do not respect it. Overspending is a lack of respect for money. Stinginess is a lack of respect for money. Once you recognize that money is an instrument that is meant to be properly handled, you will begin to understand how to properly relate to money and use it for the purpose God has ordained.

Reflection Questions

1. The Bible says that the love of money is the root of all evil. What does this mean?
2. Why do so many Christians believe that money is evil? What does the Bible actually say about money?

3. What relationship should a believer have with money and finances?
4. What is mammon? Why does the Bible say it is dangerous?

Prosperity Prayer

If you can identify with my testimony of being delivered from the love of money or if you realize your need to be delivered from the stronghold of money, then I want you to pray this prayer.

Father, in the name of Jesus, I recognize that everything in this world belongs to You. I recognize that You are an all-benevolent Father. All good things come from You. I ask that You forgive me for wrongly prioritizing and misappropriating money in my mind, heart, and life. I recognize that anything that comes before You is an idol. I renounce every idol in my life, including the idol of money. I repent for putting my needs, wants, and concerns above Your will and purpose for my life. Your Word declares that you give me the power to get wealth in order to establish Your covenant. Therefore, I receive the grace to steward wealth in a way that advances Your kingdom and brings Your name glory in Jesus's name. Amen!

12

PROSPERING IN THE END TIMES

Then you shall see and become radiant,
And your heart shall swell with joy;
Because the abundance of the sea shall be turned
    to you,
The wealth of the Gentiles shall come to you.
The multitude of camels shall cover your land,
The dromedaries of Midian and Ephah;
All those from Sheba shall come;
They shall bring gold and incense,
And they shall proclaim the praises of the Lord.
All the flocks of Kedar shall be gathered together
    to you,
The rams of Nebaioth shall minister to you;
They shall ascend with acceptance on My altar,
And I will glorify the house of My glory.

—Isaiah 60:5–7

Throughout this book, we have proven biblically and practically that it is the unconditional will of God to prosper His children. However, this book is not just about prosperity but about revival. The end-time revival that is sweeping the nations is not just about great worship services; it is a shift in the paradigm of the church and the manifestation of the glory of God in a tangible way. This outpouring of the glory will not just involve weeping and crying but will include the outpouring of great wealth on the body of Christ.

Surprisingly, many pastors and leaders omit the aspect of prosperity when they speak about revival. As mentioned above, Isaiah 60:6 is very clear. One of the signs given in Scripture of the light of God's glory shining in the earth is the Gentiles (the ungodly) bringing their wealth to the house of God. Can you imagine what this will look like?

The Joseph Mandate Revisited

Earlier in the book, we talked about the Joseph mandate for the church. We looked at the three Josephs in Scripture as a prophetic prototype for the church in the last days. Each Joseph represents a dimension of God's supernatural provision that will manifest in the last days. God's will is for us to flourish in the end times so we can facilitate the spreading of the gospel and the discipling of nations in the four corners of the earth, especially in the marketplace.

God is raising up marketplace ministers and revivalists who will use the wisdom of God to obtain great wealth, which, in turn, will finance the next great move of God. He will anoint men and women to use their resources to advance the kingdom of God. This will require radical faith, radical obedience, and radical giving. We will have to rethink money on a very fundamental level. In fact, we must reevaluate our entire lives. The existential question must be asked: "Why am I here?"

If millions of Christians discovered their purpose and committed to establishing that purpose in their respective spheres of influence, what an impact they would have! Revival does not start on a macro scale but on a micro level. When we look at the record of Scripture, 120 were in the upper room before there were 3,000 at the altar call in Acts 2.

God is raising up a remnant in the earth who will submit fully to His agenda. We must be willing to submit our resources to God so He can use them as an instrument in His hand to accomplish His divine purposes. It is not happening; it has already begun! Are you prepared? Are you willing to be part of this next great move of God? We are not waiting on God; He is waiting on us to comply.

The Pattern of Goshen

Honestly, when we look at society today, we see many things transpiring. There seems to be a shaking in the economy of the world. There is uncertainty about the future. Millions of people are unemployed or under-employed globally. Many are experiencing an economic famine. There is a global resetting of the Babylonian economic system with great collateral damage due to this shaking. Notice that I said the Babylonian system—not the church—is shaking.

Let me define the Babylonian economic system. In 2019, God began to speak to me about what He called the Babylonian economy. This is a conglomerate of evil men who have exercised control over the world financial systems, including global banks and lending institutions. These people, under the influence of demonic powers, have used their wealth and power to oppress the poor and push their nefarious agendas in society, government, and culture for centuries. However, the divine hand of God is shaking their system. This is not new. We have seen this historically and in Scripture.

During the time of Israel's sojourn in Egypt, they lived in a place called Goshen. In Genesis 25, the Hebrew people relocated to Goshen under the oversight of Joseph. By the time God responded to the cry of the children of Israel (to let them go), they were still living in Goshen. As God judged Egypt (politically, culturally, and economically), the Israelites were unaffected by those plagues.

The word *Goshen* means "drawing near."[1] God is calling the church to draw near to Him in intimacy and obedience like never before. God nourished the Israelites during the famine in Genesis. Goshen was God's answer to poverty during that time. The same is true in this prophetic season. God is raising a spiritual Goshen on the earth, a place of intimacy and supernatural provision. When the shaking hits the earth, it will not shake Goshen. God has created a supernatural canopy that will cover the believer in times of financial hardship and crisis. He will raise up business people, entrepreneurs, who are spiritual, revelatory, and sensitive to the voice of God. He will direct how their businesses interact with churches and ministries all over the world.

God wants to make you a Goshen in this hour. You are called to be a canopy of financial protection for God's people in the last days. I am reminded of the Green Family who own Hobby Lobby. They are actually billionaires. They have helped churches and, in some cases, paid off their debts. God doesn't just want to use the Green family; He wants to use you too. Glory to God!

Occupy until I Come

As I said before, one of the most detrimental things to a believer's life is wrong theology. Theology comes from two Greek words, *theos* and *logos*.[2] *Theology* is the words that God says about Himself. When your theology is wrong, it inevitably creates a wrong perception about who God is. Biblical illiteracy and biblical error are very dangerous. Not only should we be mindful of a wrong theology, but we should more specifically be concerned with a wrong eschatology (the study of end times).

If you do not have a victorious eschatological view, then you will not know how to correctly posture yourself in the last days. Many Christians are waiting for Jesus to come back while they sit on their blessed assurance because they have a wrong eschatological view. Jesus told us to occupy until He comes, not hide in a bunker while the world goes to hell in a handbasket. We are called to advance His kingdom in every sphere of society, culture, and politics.

A poor eschatological understanding led to a passive and docile church during the Holocaust. Some Christians were probably saying that the church shouldn't be involved in politics and war—while their Jewish brothers and sisters were being marched off to the gas chambers. I do not mean to be offensive, but we are at a spiritual crossroads. Either the church will affect change in society, or we will become the victims of a spiritually compromised culture. Jesus told a parable to His disciples.

> Now as they heard these things, He spoke another parable, because He was near Jerusalem and because they thought the kingdom of God would appear immediately. Therefore He said: "A certain nobleman went into a far country to receive for himself a kingdom and to return. So he called ten of his servants, delivered to them ten minas, and said to them, 'Do business till I come.'"
>
> —Luke 19:11–13

The word *occupy* comes from the Greek word *pragmateuomai*, which means "to carry on a business."[3] We are called to carry on the business of the kingdom of God in the absence of the King (although the King is not absent spiritually). We have been commissioned to be salt and light in the culture. In a military sense, we have been equipped and empowered to gain ground. God truly wants us to colonize the culture with the kingdom of God. He wants us to set up shop on the earth and expand and scale the business of the kingdom of God by spreading the gospel.

What Are You Waiting For?

It is bad theology and eschatology for us to stand on the mountain top and wait for the coming of Jesus while the world burns. We can't do that! In a very real sense, we have been given responsibility over what happens on this planet. You might be thinking, *That sounds like Kingdom Now theology.* You can call it whatever you want, but Jesus left the church on earth for a reason, and it wasn't to warm the pews.

Carl's Jr. Corporation was started by one person, and now they have thirty-eight thousand locations. They did this by occupying territory in the marketplace and expanding the vision of their original founder. Maybe a burger restaurant has more revelation than the church in this area. But when we look at the early church, we can clearly see that they understood the mandate Jesus gave them.

> Go therefore and make disciples of all the nations, baptizing them in the name of the Father and of the Son and of the Holy Spirit, teaching them to observe all things that I have commanded you; and lo, I am with you always, even to the end of the age. Amen.
>
> —Matthew 28:19–20

Jesus sent His disciples in the Great Commission to teach or disciple all nations. We cannot disciple nations if we don't move out of our comfort zones. We cannot disciple nations if we do not have any resources. We are called to tell every creature on earth that Jesus is coming back with the confirmation of signs, wonders, and miracles. But we must also have the resources to facilitate this Great Commission.

Every major religion in the world uses business and enterprise to spread its agenda. The only exception is the

Christian Church. Many in the church are busy thinking that money is evil. We cannot accumulate what we are constantly rebuking. God has called us to use the resources He has entrusted to us to propagate the gospel and train nations to operate in the kingdom of God in preparation for the great second coming of our Lord Jesus.

What are you waiting for? He wants us to plant churches, raise up leaders, and send out people to make disciples in every nation. We must have the resources to ensure that the gospel is spreading rapidly.

What Are You Doing Right Now?

During the pandemic, God grew our ministry supernaturally; our congregation grew by nearly 70 percent. We grew financially. We built a bakery and a studio when many churches were closing down. We gave away hundreds of thousands of dollars to benevolence and missions. We decided that the Word of God was true regardless of circumstances. God told me to raise up a Joseph Business Group (a community of successful entrepreneurs that would sow into the church and support revival). This is just the beginning.

God is about to release billions to the body of Christ. But these billions are not coming to the fearful, the idle, or the lazy. He is releasing these resources to people who are already doing something now. He wants people who are advancing the kingdom of God right now within their spheres of influence. So much needs to be done. So many lives need to be saved. So many people have never tangibly experienced the love of God. We have been given the keys to the kingdom of God. Will you use them? It is time to stop making excuses. There is a place called now, and that is the place of unlimited prosperity.

God wants you to prosper and have good success. He wants your life to flourish so that the people around you can see and experience His goodness through your life. He has empowered you and anointed your hands to obtain wealth so that you can establish His covenant on earth. What are you doing right now? What are you doing with your time? What are you doing with your talents? What are you doing with your treasures? This will determine how much more God can release to you.

Moving to 777 Abundance Avenue

We are living in the most important times in human history, but we must be discerning and diligent. God wants to teach you how to prosper just like He taught me, but it will require humility and persistence. You must be willing to completely stop making excuses and to stop playing the blame game and embrace the law of generosity. You must be willing to activate the law of seedtime and harvest in every area of your life. Through the teaching in this book, God will break the back of generational poverty off your life and the lives of everyone connected to you.

Release your faith now for the abundant life that God has graciously provided for you in Christ. It is a life of victory and joy. You no longer have to live broke, busted, and disgusted. You are changing addresses and moving from 666 Poverty Place to 777 Abundance Avenue. Are you ready to make the shift? Now is the time. Today is the day. You will never live in the place of lack another day in your life in the name of Jesus. Amen!

Reflection Questions

1. What is God's end-time plan concerning finances? What does this plan look like?
2. What is the spiritual significance of Goshen for believers today? Why is this a critical truth?
3. What did Jesus mean when He said, "Occupy until I come!"?
4. How do we practically disciple nations? What are we called to teach these nations?

Prosperity Prayer

Father, in the name of Jesus, I thank You for who You are and for all that You have done in my life. Lord, I know that You are the God of more than enough, and because of You, I have everything that I need. Father, it is Your sovereign will that I flourish in every area of my life—including my finances. I declare that wealth and riches are in my house, according to Psalm 112:3. I declare that I am a kingdom financer and that You cause whatever I touch to prosper in the name of Jesus. I declare that I am a storehouse for the poor, fatherless, and widow. I declare that I am an end-time ambassador for the kingdom of God. I declare that heaven partners with me to distribute spiritual and physical resources to those in need. Thank You, Father, for Your supernatural favor and abundance that flows freely in and through my life for Your glory. In the mighty name of Jesus, I pray. Amen!

ACKNOWLEDGMENTS

I want to first and foremost give God all the glory for His grace and love toward me. I want to acknowledge my wife and her valuable insights as a tremendous gift that God has given me. I want to acknowledge the publishing and editing staff of Chosen Books and Baker Publishing Group (including David Sluka and Kate Jameson, and many more) for publishing this message and presenting it in an excellent way. To my staff, thank you for all of your diligence and hard work.

NOTES

Chapter 1 "God's Purpose for Prosperity"

1. "Lexicon :: Strong's H6509 – *pārâ*," Blue Letter Bible, accessed February 24, 2024, https://www.blueletterbible.org/lexicon/h6509/kjv/wlc/0-1/.

2. *Oxford English Dictionary*, s.v. "fruitful (*adj.*)," accessed February 24, 2024, https://www.oed.com/search/dictionary/?scope=Entries&q=fruitful; *Merriam-Webster Dictionary*, s.v. "fruitful (*adj.*)," accessed February 24, 2024, https://www.merriam-webster.com/dictionary/fruitful.

3. "Definition of *fertilis*," Latin Lexicon, accessed February 24, 2024, https://latinlexicon.org/definition.php?p1=2022133&p2=f.

4. Encyclopedia, s.v. "toil (*n.*)," accessed February 24, 2024, https://www.encyclopedia.com/humanities/dictionaries-thesauruses-pictures-and-press-releases/toil-0.

5. "Lexicon :: Strong's H5647 – *'ābad*," Blue Letter Bible, accessed February 24, 2024, https://www.blueletterbible.org/lexicon/h5647/kjv/wlc/0-1/.

6. "Lexicon :: Strong's H8104 – *šāmar*," Blue Letter Bible, accessed February 24, 2024, https://www.blueletterbible.org/lexicon/h8104/kjv/wlc/0-1/.

7. Myles Munroe, *Rediscovering the Kingdom* (Shippensburg, PA: Destiny Image Publishers, 2004), 97.

8. "Lexicon :: Strong's H3581 – *kōaḥ*," Blue Letter Bible, accessed February 24, 2024, https://www.blueletterbible.org/lexicon/h3581/kjv/wlc/0-1/.

Chapter 2 "Even as Your Soul Prospers"

1. "Lexicon :: Strong's H7965 – *šālôm*," Blue Letter Bible, accessed February 24, 2024, https://www.blueletterbible.org/lexicon/h7965/kjv/wlc/0-1/.

2. *Oxford English Dictionary*, s.v. "debt (*n*.)," accessed February 24, 2024, https://www.oed.com/search/dictionary/?scope=Entries&q=debt.

3. Latin-Dictionary, s.v. "debitum, debiti, (*n*).," accessed February 29, 2024, https://latin-dictionary.net/definition/15704/debitum-debiti#:~:text=Definitions%3A,debt%2Fwhat%20is%20owed.

4. "Lexicon :: Strong's G3007 – *leipō*," Blue Letter Bible, February 24, 2024, https://www.blueletterbible.org/lexicon/g3007/kjv/tr/0-1/.

5. "Lexicon :: Strong's G2344 – *thēsauros*," Blue Letter Bible, accessed February 24, 2024, https://www.blueletterbible.org/lexicon/g2344/kjv/tr/0-1/.

Chapter 3 "Poverty, the Destiny Thief"

1. "Lexicon :: Strong's G2222 – *zōē*," Blue Letter Bible, accessed February 24, 2024, https://www.blueletterbible.org/lexicon/g2222/kjv/tr/0-1/.

2. "Lexicon :: Strong's H5046 – *nāḡaḏ*," Blue Letter Bible, accessed February 24, 2024, https://www.blueletterbible.org/lexicon/h5046/kjv/wlc/0-1/.

3. "Lexicon :: Strong's H7999 – *šālam*," Blue Letter Bible, accessed February 24, 2024, https://www.blueletterbible.org/lexicon/h7999/kjv/wlc/0-1/.

4. Melody K. Smith, "What Systemic Poverty Looks Like May Surprise You," Presbyterian Mission, December 11, 2020, https://www.presbyterianmission.org/story/what-systemic-poverty-looks-like-may-surprise-you/.

5. "Lexicon :: Strong's G2616 – *katadynasteuō*," Blue Letter Bible, accessed February 24, 2024, https://www.blueletterbible.org/lexicon/g2616/kjv/tr/0-1/.

6. "Lexicon :: Strong's G1413 – *dynastēs*," Blue Letter Bible, accessed February 24, 2024, https://www.blueletterbible.org/lexicon/g1413/kjv/tr/0-1/.

7. Google Dictionary, s.v. "dynasty (*n*.)," accessed February 24, 2024, https://googledictionary.freecollocation.com/meaning?word=dynasty.

Chapter 4 "The Joseph Mandate"

1. "Lexicon :: Strong's H3084 – *yᵊhôsēp̄*," Blue Letter Bible, accessed February 24, 2024, https://www.blueletterbible.org/lexicon /h3084/kjv/wlc/0-1/.

2. "Lexicon :: Strong's G2424 – *iēsous*," Blue Letter Bible, accessed February 24, 2024, https://www.blueletterbible.org/lexicon/g2424/kjv /tr/0-1/.

3. "Lexicon :: Strong's G707 – *arimathaia*," Blue Letter Bible, accessed February 24, 2024, https://www.blueletterbible.org/lexicon /g707/kjv/tr/0-1/.

Chapter 5 "Real versus False Prosperity"

1. "Lexicon :: Strong's H6965 – *qûm*," Blue Letter Bible, accessed February 24, 2024, https://www.blueletterbible.org/lexicon/h6965/kjv /wlc/0-1/.

2. "Significant Statistics about Tithing and Church Generosity," CDF Capital, February 25, 2019, https://www.cdfcapital.org/tithing -generosity/.

3. Leonardo Blair, "Only 13% of Evangelicals Tithe, Half Give Away Less Than 1% of Income Annually: Study," Christian Post, October 29, 2021, https://www.christianpost.com/news/only-13-of -evangelicals-tithe-study.html.

4. "What Is a Tithe? New Data on Perceptions of the 10 Percent," Barna Group, September 7, 2022, https://www.barna.com/research /what-is-a-tithe/.

Chapter 6 "The Power of Blessing"

1. "Lexicon :: Strong's G2127 – *eulogeō*," Blue Letter Bible, February 24, 2024, https://www.blueletterbible.org/lexicon/g2127/kjv/tr/0-1/.

2. "Lexicon :: Strong's G1746 – *endyō*," Blue Letter Bible, accessed February 24, 2024, https://www.blueletterbible.org/lexicon/g1746/kjv /tr/0-1/.

3. "Lexicon :: Strong's G5241 – *hyperentygchanō*," Blue Letter Bible, accessed February 24, 2024, https://www.blueletterbible.org /lexicon/g5241/kjv/tr/0-1/.

4. *Oxford Learner's Dictionary*, s.v. "decree (*n.*)," accessed February 29, 2024, https://www.oxfordlearnersdictionaries.com/us/defin ition/english/decree_1.

5. "Lexicon :: Strong's H1504 – *gāzar*," Blue Letter Bible, accessed February 24, 2024, https://www.blueletterbible.org/lexicon/h1504/nasb20/wlc/0-1/.

6. "Lexicon :: Strong's G2127 – *eulogeō*," Blue Letter Bible, February 24, 2024, https://www.blueletterbible.org/lexicon/g2127/kjv/tr/0-1/.

Chapter 7 "The Law of Seedtime and Harvest and Cooperating with the Spirit of Divine Increase"

1. "Lexicon :: Strong's G5485 – *charis*," Blue Letter Bible, accessed February 29, 2024, https://www.blueletterbible.org/lexicon/g5485/kjv/tr/0-1/.

Chapter 8 "Tired of Being Sick and Tired and Renouncing the Vow of Poverty"

1. *Oxford English Dictionary*, s.v. "paradigm (*n.*)," accessed February 24, 2024, https://www.oed.com/search/dictionary/?q=paradigm.

2. "Lexicon :: Strong's G3339 – *metamorphoō*," Blue Letter Bible, accessed February 24, 2024, https://www.blueletterbible.org/lexicon/g3339/kjv/tr/0-1/.

3. "Lexicon :: Strong's G342 – *anakainōsis*," Blue Letter Bible, accessed February 24, 2024, https://www.blueletterbible.org/lexicon/g342/kjv/tr/0-1/.

4. "Lexicon :: Strong's G2807 – *kleis*," Blue Letter Bible, accessed February 29, 2024, https://www.blueletterbible.org/lexicon/g2807/kjv/tr/0-1/.

5. "Lexicon :: Strong's G1210 – *deō*," Blue Letter Bible, accessed February 29, 2024, https://www.blueletterbible.org/lexicon/g1210/kjv/tr/0-1/.

6. "Lexicon :: Strong's G3089 – *lyō*," Blue Letter Bible, accessed February 29, 2024, https://www.blueletterbible.org/lexicon/g3089/kjv/tr/0-1/.

7. "Lexicon :: Strong's G936 – *basileuō*," Blue Letter Bible, February 29, 2024, https://www.blueletterbible.org/lexicon/g936/kjv/tr/0-1/.

Chapter 9 "Seeking First the Kingdom of God"

1. *Britannica*, s.v. "ambassador (*n.*)," accessed February 29, 2024, https://www.britannica.com/topic/ambassador.

Chapter 10 "Why Am I Broke? Asking the *Hard* Questions"

1. "Number of Masters Tournament titles from 1934 to 2022, by player," Statista, accessed February 29, 2024, https://www.statista.com/statistics/222030/golf-players-with-the-most-victories-at-the-masters-tournament/#:~:text=The%20ranking%20shows%20golf%20players,Jack%20Nicklaus%20with%20six%20wins.

2. *Oxford Reference*, s.v. "parable (*n.*)," accessed February 29, 2024, https://www.oxfordreference.com/display/10.1093/oi/authority.20110803100304891.

Chapter 11 "The Love of Money . . ."

1. "Lexicon :: Strong's H1897 – *hāgâ*," Blue Letter Bible, accessed February 29, 2024, https://www.blueletterbible.org/lexicon/h1897/kjv/wlc/0-1/.

2. "Lexicon :: Strong's G94 – *adikos*," Blue Letter Bible, accessed February 29, 2024, https://www.blueletterbible.org/lexicon/g94/kjv/tr/0-1/.

3. "Lexicon :: Strong's G1349 – *dike*," Blue Letter Bible accessed February 29, 2024, https://www.blueletterbible.org/lexicon/g1349/kjv/tr/0-1/.

4. "Lexicon :: Strong's H3581 – *kōaḥ*," Blue Letter Bible, accessed February 24, 2024, https://www.blueletterbible.org/lexicon/h3581/kjv/wlc/0-1/.

Chapter 12 "Prospering in the End Times"

1. "Lexicon :: Strong's H1657 – *gōšen*," Blue Letter Bible, accessed February 29, 2024, https://www.blueletterbible.org/lexicon/h1657/kjv/wlc/0-1/.

2. "Lexicon :: Strong's G2316 – *theos*," Blue Letter Bible, accessed February 29, 2024, https://www.blueletterbible.org/lexicon/g2316/kjv/tr/0-1/; "Lexicon :: Strong's G3056 – *logos*," Blue Letter Bible, accessed February 29, 2024, https://www.blueletterbible.org/lexicon/g3056/kjv/tr/0-1/.

3. "Lexicon :: Strong's G4231 – *pragmateuomai*," Blue Letter Bible, accessed February 29, 2024, https://www.blueletterbible.org/lexicon/g4231/kjv/tr/0-1/.

Dr. Kynan Bridges is a dynamic teacher, pastor, and conference speaker. His television broadcast, *Your Miraculous Life*, on Daystar Television reaches 1.3 billion homes every week. His social media platform has 1.4 million followers and reaches 250 million accounts every week. He is the published author of more than twenty-three books, many of which are bestselling titles. He pastors a growing church in Tampa with several thousand attendees online and in person. Dr. Kynan Bridges is a committed husband to Gloria Bridges and the father of six beautiful children.